Battleground Europe

TOURING THE ITALIAN FRONT
1917-1918

British, American, French & German
Forces in Northern Italy

Battleground Europe

TOURING THE ITALIAN FRONT
1917-1918
British, American, French & German
Forces in Northern Italy

Francis Mackay

LEO COOPER

For the descendants of those who fought in Italy during the Great War, in the hope that it will help them follow the footsteps of an earlier generation.

First published in 2002 by
LEO COOPER
an imprint of
Pen & Sword Books Limited
47 Church Street, Barnsley, South Yorkshire, S70 2AS

Copyright © Francis Mackay
ISBN 0 85052 876 3

A CIP catalogue record of this book is available
from the British Library

Printed by CPI UK.

For up-to-date information on other titles produced under the Leo Cooper imprint, please telephone or write to:

Pen & Sword Books Ltd, FREEPOST, 47 Church Street
Barnsley, South Yorkshire S70 2AS
Telephone 01226 734555

CONTENTS

Introduction by Series Editor

After the disaster of Caporetto in late 1917 Britain and France despatched substantial numbers of troops to the Italian Front to help to shore up the severely shaken Italian army. In fact, by the time that these troops arrived, the Italians had regained control of the situation and re-established a stable front. However, the arrival of these allied troops was a significant boost to morale both of the Italian army and of the nation as a whole, and an indication that the needs of Italy would not be ignored by her northern allies. Later on, a brigade sized detachment of American troops was added to the allied force.

This is not to say that these troops did nothing apart from reassure by their presence; they were involved in defending the line against a determined Austro-Hungarian assault in June 1918 and in the series of actions preceding the Austrian Armistice. The conditions were vastly different to those endured by the British on the Western Front - not least in the nature of the mountainous countryside, the wide rivers, the climate (both colder and hotter, in due season) and the same scale. It should also give cause for reflection about the whole of the Italian Campaign; of those brave and long-suffering Italian and Austro-Hungarian soldiers who battled in the most extreme of conditions for several years.

It is a difficult task covering such a significant area of norther Italy in a guide, expecially as there is so little English that is readily available to help the tourist or pilgrim. Francis MacKay has managed to come up with an imaginative series of tour routes, supplemented with a range of introductions to explain the context: no mean task. Unlike other *Battleground Europe* books it will be essential to equip yourself with good local maps, as suggested in the text, fortunately, quite readily available. The Italians boast some very good war museums, as I have seen myself at Rovereto. There are substantial remnants of the war still be found in northern Italy, and time spent here can only be an eye-opener to those who think of British military operations solely in the context of the Western Front. He has also found the space to spend time on each of the other combatants, but almost particularly the French and the Americans.

This will be an invaluable book for those coming to Italy for the first time on the trail of the soldiers of the BEF who found themselves - very unexpectedly - in the beautiful country of the Asiago and Piave. It is well past time they, too, received a steady flow of visitors to wonder at their perseverance and tenacity.

Nigel Cave - *Villa Bolangaro, Stresa*

Acknowledgements

Crown Copyright is reproduced with the permission of the Controller of Her Majesty's Stationery Office. I am grateful to the following persons or organisations. The Regimental Archive of the Oxford & Buckinghamshire Light Infantry for photographs, and information about the raid on Sec, and especially to Richard Jeffs, the Honorary Archivist, for help and enthusiastic support. Stuart Eastwood, Curator, Regimental Museum, King's Own Border Regiment, Carlisle Castle, for information about the life and death of Lieutenant Colonel W W Kerr, and to the Trustees of the Museum for permission to quote from *The Border Regiment in the Great War*. Donatella Castello, *Il Capo Servizio*, Comune di Malo, and Gasparella Priabona, *Centro Studi del Priabona*, Comune di Malo di Monte, for assistance and a generous gift of books and photographs about the Great War and their home-towns, including the story of Dom Raumer and his diary. Stewart Gilbert, Editor, *Berrow's Worcester Journal*, the world's oldest newspaper, for permission to quote from Edward Corbett's book about the 1/8th Battalion The Worcestershire Regiment, sadly long out of print. Lieutenant Colonel Pat Love, Honorary Archivist, RHQ, The Worcestershire Regiment, for information, advice and encouragement. Sr Marzio Bomitali of BericaEditrice, for assistance with maps and mapping; the Emo family for permission to use the photograph of the Villa Emo. Laurie Pettitt for copious information about awards to British servicemen during the campaign. Thanks especially to Alex Blanning, Peter Brooks, Katriona Coutts, Maryon Fairman, Roger Garbett, Peter Grudgings, Frank Jameson, June Page and David Thistlethwaite for permission to use information, photographs or recollections of their relatives' service in Italy. Dale Hjort for the provision of photographs, information and advice. My particular thanks to Stefania Rigoni, of the Ufficio del Turismo, Città di Asiago, for endless patience in dealing with requests for information and translation of obscure documents. Oriella Paccanaro, L'Assessore di Turismo, Comune di Montecchio Maggiore for maps and permission to have them published.

Dr Vincenzo Calì, Direttore, *Museo Storica Delle Guerra, Rovereto*, for permission to use the photograph of that splendid establishment. My particular thanks go to Mauro and Lucilla Agostinetto, custodians of the German Military Cemetery, Quero, for their assistance and patience.

Despite numerous efforts, I have been unable to contact any descendants of Battalion Sergeant Major Joseph Lettau regarding his interesting and useful book about the life and times of the 332nd Infantry Regiment; perhaps this guide will lead me to them.

Introduction

The aim of this guide is to introduce battlefield tourists active and armchair, genealogists, families of veterans, and anyone interested in the Italian Campaign, to locations in northern Italy where British, French, US and German troops served during the final years of the Great War.

This guide was compiled from rough notes made 'on the hoof' during many battlefield visits with NATO colleagues. Many of these obtained information from their national archives or staff colleges to assist in our explorations. Information arrived by telephone, fax, e-mail or letter, usually without references, as I had no intention then of writing a guide-book. Hence my caveats of 'possibly', 'probably', etc. If anyone can amend or correct anything written here then their contribution will be very welcome.

There is still much to be written about the Italian campaign, an under-rated episode in the Great War. Historians may come to revise the general view expressed by the author of *The Seventh Divison 1914-1918,* lamenting *that it was strange that a Divison with the Seventh's record should have been stranded in a backwater during the greatest crisis of the war* [the March 1918 Offensive].

This guide covers only a few episodes in a complex and unusual campaign, fought on battlegrounds ranging from the Venetian lagoons to Dolomite peaks. The wider story of the Italian campaign can be read in the *Official History of the War, Military Operations, Italy 1915-1919* (James Edmonds), *The British Army in Italy 1917-1919* and *Rommel and Caporetto* (both by John and Eileen Wilks), and *The Forgotten Front, The British Army in Italy 1917-1918*, (George Cassar). A previous Battleground guide, *Asiago, 15/16 June 1918, The Battle in the Woods and Clouds,* covers the role of British troops in the Battle of the Piave.

Foreword
by
Lieutenant Colonel Taylor Voorhis Beattie
US Special Forces

LTC Taylor Beattie USA

Like most professional soldiers I enjoy exploring old battlefields. There is a great sense of history and, oddly, peace, to be found in the silent trenches and battlefields of the Great War.

During 2001, while on military business in Northern Italy, I explored the Asiago battlefields with Francis Mackay's previous guide, dog-eared and much underlined, as my indispensable companion. *Touring the Italian Front* British, French, American and German Forces in Italy, 1917-1918, is a worthy successor to *Asiago*, and I am particularly pleased to see coverage of much of the almost unknown part played in the campaign by my fellow countrymen. Their story is unknown in the USA outside a handful of enthusiasts, and I long to know more about those men from Ohio and West Virginia (and other states of the Union) who served on the Venetian plain in 1918.

I commend this book to potential tourists to the battlegrounds of the Italian Front and hope that you will pause to reflect on the soldiers of all nations who fought and died there, and whose memory, deeds and devotions still inspire.

Taylor Voorhis Beattie
Lieutenant Colonel, Special Forces
US Army

Advice for Tourists

Access. As of Spring 2002 the locations described here were not suitable for tourists with restricted mobility.

Location: Most of the locations described here lie within two hours of Vicenza, a beautiful city, little known to British and American tourists, but popular with several generations of American, British and French servicemen.

Maps: A good road atlas of North East Italy is vital. The Litografia Artistica Cartografica (LAC) Carta della Provincia (Provincial Maps) of Verona, Vicenza, Treviso and Padua [Padova] noted in tour itineraries are usually available from The Map Shop, Upton on Severn, (0800 085 40 80, *www.themapshop.co.uk*), or Stanfords, Covent Garden, London, WC2E 9LP (020 7836 1321, *www.stanfords.co.uk*). The small but efficient cartographic house of BericEditrice produces excellent 1:20,000 maps, with English footnotes, for the Montello and the Colli Vicentini; in late 2002 they were only available outside Italy by on-line purchasing via *www.vialesport.com*. The *Azienda di Promozione Turistica Asiago – 7 Comuni* can provide an excellent 1:30,000 Great War Tourist Map (I Luoghi Della Grande Guerra 1915-1918) of the Asiago Plateau; (see below for the address).

A small compass is handy when walking in the forests of the Asiago Plateau.

Air Travel: Venice, Treviso and Verona are served by scheduled and charter services from the UK, and Venice and Milan by connecting flights from the US.

Driving: Check with the AA/AAA, RAC, etc about Italian motoring regulations and driving advice. Italian drivers rarely stop at pedestrian crossings, not out of impoliteness, it is just the way things are done in Italy, but it all seems to work.

Work was due to start in mid-2002 on a new autostrada running from the A4 west of Vicenza to the A27 north-east of Treviso, so be alert for exit and entry points not mentioned here.

Forest roads on the Asiago Plateau may be closed at any time due to logging operations; a red and white disc at the side of the track means 'Keep Out', and the Forest Guards (members of the *Corpo Forestale dello Stato*) enforce such bans with firm courtesy in the interests of safety.

Trains: Vicenza can be reached via Milan, or from Munich via Verona; some trains run on to Padua and Venice. Local trains connect Vicenza and Padua to Thiene, Cittadella, Bassano del Grappa and Treviso from where buses run to many of the locations mentioned in this guide.

Mountain Bike: Ideal for exploring most of this area, especially the Montello, the Asiago area, and the Piave shore line; check with local tourist boards about hire. *Montagnaveneta.com* lists tours of the Montello, among other locations.

Weather: Veneto summers are hot, humid and smoggy. Late May/early June, mid-September/early October, and early November can be cool and clear, especially the Summer of St Martin, around 11 November.

The escarpment backing the Venetian Plain, including Monte Grappa and Monfenera, is cool in autumn and spring, and can quickly become wreathed in rolling mist, even in summer, so be prepared. Rain in the area is torrential by UK standards.

Tourist Offices: The Italian Embassy or Consulate should be able to supply an up-to-date list of tourist offices covering the Veneto, or try the website – *www.regione.veneto.it*.

Comune di Asiago: Ufficio del Turismo, Piazza Carli, 36012, Asiago (VI). Tel: +39 0424 464081, fax: +39 0424 463885.
e-mail: *asiagoturismo@comune.asiago.vi.it* website: *www.comune.asiago.vi.it*

Altopiano di Asiago: Azienda di Promozione Turistica, Via Stazione 5, 36012, Asiago (VI). Tel: +39 0424 462221, fax: +39 0424 462445.
e-mail: *apt-asiago@ascom.vi.it* website: *www.ascom.vi.it/asiago/*

Colli Euganei: Ente Parco Regionale dei Colli Euganei, via Fontana 2, 35032, Arquà Petrarca (PD.) Tel: +39 0429 777145, fax: +39 0429 777144. e-mail/website: *www.collieuganei.com.*

Montebelluna: Treviso APT, Via Toniolo 41, Palazzo Scotti, 31100, Treviso (VI). Tel: +39 0422 540600, fax: +39 0422 541397.
e-mail: *tvapt@sevenonline.it* website: *www.sevenonline.it/tvapt.*

Padua: Azienda di Promozione Turistica, Riviera di Mugnai 8, 35137, Padova. Tel: +39 049 8750655, fax: +39 049 650794.
e-mail: *apt-08@mail.regione.veneto.it* website: *www.padova.it/apt.*

Vicenza: Azienda di Promozione Turistica, Piazza Duomo 5, 36100, Vicenza. Tel: +39 0444 544122, fax: +39 0444 325001.
e-mail: *apt-10@mail.regione.veneto.it*
website: *www.ascom.vi.it/aptvicenza*

Verona: Azienda di Promozione Turistica, Piazza Delle Erbe 38, 37121, Verona. Tel: +39 0458 000065, fax: +39 0458 010682.
e-mail: *apt-13@mail.reghione.veneto.it*
website: *www.tourism.verona.it*

Trento: Azienda per la Promozione Turistica, Via Alfieri 4, 38100, Trento. Tel: +39 0461 983880, fax: +39 0461984508.
e-mail: *informazione@apt.trento* website: *www.apt.trento.it*

Camping and Caravan sites: *www.camping.it*

Self-catering: Scarce outside the Asiago Plateau. In Asiago the Sporting Residence (apartments) is known to be comfortable and well equipped with an indoor swimming pool.

Apartments: Singles for one to nine people. *www.sportingasiago.com,* a list of other self-catering accommodation is available from the Tourist Office.

Battlefield Tours: Flanders Tours, (+44 01480 890966, *www.flandertours.com*), Tours With Experts Ltd, (+44 0151 526 0075, *www.tours-with-experts.com*), and the War Research Society (+44 0121 430 5348, *www.battlefieldtours.co.uk*) take an interest in the Veneto.

Health: As far as can be determined, within the area covered by this guide, only the Ospedale Civile, Vicenza, has a 24-hour English-speaking duty physician service.

Safety: Keep out of dug-outs. Do not pick up anything remotely like a bomb, bullet, grenade, shell or cartridge case. The green, tumbling rivers of the Veneto look tempting on a humid day in high summer,

An irrigation channel.... cold, fast and dangerous. FM

but they are bitterly cold, and sudden immersion can be traumatic. Be very careful, even if paddling, as the current is swift, the channels deceptively deep and the bed slippery. Do not attempt to paddle or swim in an irrigation channel. Apart from legal aspects, the current is swift and powerful, the water bitterly cold and the sloping concrete sides provide no grip.

Danger: Check with your hotel, or a riverside café, about swimming or paddling in the Piave between Quero and Ponte Priùla as apparently that reach has a peculiar underwater hazard – areas of 'sinking stones', where paddlers, or people wading after swimming, can plunge, becoming trapped under the shingle and drown. These are probably springs in the river bed, and one source claims they appear and disappear at random.

Food and drink: Most cafés and food shops close on Mondays. Italians find the idea of visitors eating their own food in a café odd, to say the least. To avoid unintentional offence keep picnics for picnic places, and cafés for coffee.

Language: Few people in the Veneto outside the main tourist areas speak English. A good Italian-English dictionary is vital but do study the IPA/ pronunciation rules at the front; a quick guide: Montecchio – Mon-tek-yo. Maggiore – Ma-jo-ray. Giavera – Jaa-vra. Sacile – Sa-chee-lay. Dueville – Doo-ee-vee-lay. Grave – gra-vay. Piave – Pee-aa-vay.

CWGC: (Commonwealth War Graves Commission) Cemeteries. For anyone unfamiliar with CWGC signs, they are 'pointers', painted dark green with a white border, embellished with CWGC and the name of the cemetery, and (usually) the distance in kilometres.

Cemeteries: If visiting CWGC graves in Italian civil cemeteries, note that most have restricted opening hours, a long lunch and break.

Notes

Austro-Hungary is rendered 'Austria', and that states three armies collectively as *k.u.k* [*Kaiserliches und Königliches Heer*]. M. is Monte (Mount) e.g. M. Tomba, Colli – a range of low hills, e.g. Colli Berici. A *grave* is a bed of shingle and gravel in a river which has survived the floods long enough to sprout vegetation. *Bund* is a flood containment embankment. This word appears in war diaries, and divisional and unit histories; it stems from British India, where Imperial civil engineers and surveyors coined it from the Hindi name for an earth bank – *band*. A *switch* in this case was a diagonal barbed wire barrier, sometimes in front of a trench, running between front line trenches and support (secondary) trenches designed to channel enemy break-through forces into killing zones.

Tour 'legs' are expressed in kilometres to help anyone using a hired car.

Abbreviations

National Military Headquarters:
Austrian – AOK (Armeeoberkommando)
Italian – CS (Commando Supremo; denotes both the Chief of the General Staff of the Italian Army and his HQ.)
French – GQG (Grand Quartier Gènèral)
British – WO (War Office.)

GOC: *General Officer Commanding* a major formation, such as an expeditionary force, corps, division or brigade.
Honvéd – k.u.k. units or formations of Hungarian origin.
IR: *Infantry Regiment* in the Austrian, Italian, French and US armies;

these were composed of three infantry battalions, equivalent in some ways to a British brigade in 1918; the latter had four battalions up to February of that year, but three thereafter, except in Italy where the reduction did not take place until September.

IWGC: *Imperial War Graves Commission,* predecessor of the CWGC
WD: *War Diary* of a unit (e.g. an infantry battalion) or formation (a brigade or division); daily record of events kept by either the Adjutant, the Assistant Adjutant or an officer appointed by the Commanding Officer.

Genealogy & Research

CWGC Cemetery Registers. The names of the dead and missing in North East Italy are contained in five volumes of registers in the Italy 1914-1918 series. The CWGC no longer holds supplies of these registers but copies may be obtainable from Terry Denham, PO Box 372, Haywards Heath, West Sussex, RH17 7FL. *Email: denham@dial.pipex.com.*

Italy 1-5 (one volume): Asiago Plateau; Barental, Boscon, Magnaboschi, Granezza, Cavaletto.

Italy 7: Giavera

Italy 8: The Memorial To The Missing On The Italian Front, in Giavera Cemetery.

Italy 10 and 11: Dueville and Montecchio Precalcino cemeteries

Italy 15-93: CWGC graves in Italian community cemeteries throughout Italy, including twenty-four in the north-east. Guides for areas or events not covered by this guide are: **Italy 6:** Taranto and the south; **Italy 9:** Tezze; **Italy 12, 13, 14:** Genoa and north-west Italy.

War Service: A basic Order of Battle is provided below. The Official History of the campaign contains complete Orders of Battle, including minor units, e.g. 35th Mobile Veterinary section. The composition of the corps and divisions changed in spring 1918, and that of brigades in early September 1918 (between 10-15 September) each losing one infantry battalion; * below. Regimental titles and spelling are those used during the Great War.

Researchers: Readers new to researching their forefathers or mothers service are advised to read *Army Service Records of the First World War* (see bibliography) or use the services of one of the numerous independent researchers who for a small fee will provide a brief service history, including medals and awards received. The following have been known to provide an accurate service: Ian MacCallum BEM, (CSFHS), Trelawney Cottage, The Square, Gargunnock, Stirling, FK8 3BH.

(Tel: +44[0]1786 860488, e-mail: *info@scottishancestors.co.uk).*
David Seaney, Dinedor Cross, Hereford, HR2 6PF (tel: +44 [01]432 870420.
e-mail: *sunsetmilitaria@btinternet.com).*

War Diaries: Public Record Office file numbers are shown after each formation title; battalion war diaries are sub-sets of their Brigade file.

Order of Battle – British Expeditionary Force, Italy

XI CORPS (to Western Front, Spring 1918)	WO95/4213
1/1 King Edward's Horse	WO95/4213
11/Cyclists (i.e. 11th Battalion, Army Cyclist Corps)	WO95/4213
5th Division (to Western Front, Spring 1918)	WO95/4214
Divisional troops – Pioneers: 1/6 Argyll	WO95/4215
13 Brigade: 14/ & 15/R. Warwick, 2/King's Own Scottish Borderers, 1/R. West Kent Regt	WO95/4216
15 Brigade: 16/R. Warwick, 1/Norfolk, 1/Bedford, 1/Cheshire	WO95/4217
95 Brigade: 1/Devon, 12/Gloucester, 1/East Surrey, 1/Duke of Cornwall's Light Infantry	WO95/4217
48th (South Midlands) Division (to XIV Corps Spring 1918)	WO95/4244 WO95/4245
Divisional troops – Pioneers: 1/5 R. Sussex	WO95/4246, 4247
143 Brigade: 1/5, 1/6, 1/7, 1/8 R. Warwick	WO95/4248
144 Brigade: 1/4 & 1/6 Gloucesters, 1/7 & 1/8 Worcester*	WO95/4249
145 Brigade: 1/5 Gloucester,* 1/1 Bucks Bn, 1/4 Ox & Bucks LI, 5/R Berkshire	WO95/4250 WO95/4251
XIV CORPS	WO95/4212. 4217
1/1 Northamptonshire Yeomanry	WO95/4205
14/Cyclists	WO95/4205
7th Division	WO95/4218, 4219, 4220
Divisional troops – Pioneers: 24/Manchester	WO95/4221, 4222
20 Brigade: 8/Devon, 9/Devon*, 2/Border, 2/Gordons	WO95/4223, 4224
22 Brigade: 2/R.Warwick, 1/R. Welsh Fusiliers 20/Manchester*, 2/1 HAC (Honourable Artillery Company)	WO95/4225, 4226
91 Brigade: 2/Queen's, 1/S. Staffs, 21/Manchester*, 22/Manchester	WO95/4227, 4228

23rd Division   WO95/4235, 4236
Divisional troops – Pionee s: 9/S. Staffs   WO95/4236
68 Brigade: 10/Northumberland Fu iliers, 11 F,
    12/Durham Light Infantry, 13/DLI*   WO95/4235, 4236
69 Brigade: 11/West Yorks, 8/Yorkshire Regiment,
    9/Yorks*, 10/Duke of Wellington's   WO95/4237.4238
70 Brigade: 11/Sherwood Foresters*, 8/King's
    Own Yorkshire LI, 8/York & Lancaster, 9/Y&L   WO95/4239, 4240

Note: The Yorkshire Regiment (or, to be exact – Alexandra, The Princess of Wales's Own Yorkshire Regiment, 19th of Foot) were nicknamed the Green Howards in 1744 to avoid confusion on the battlefield when two regiments were named after their Colonel – Howard's Regiment. As one Regiment wore green facings on their scarlet uniforms they were called the Green Howards, whilst the other was nicknamed the Buffs after their buff brown facings. The nickname only became official in 1920, so divisional, brigade and battalion War Diaries and Battle Narratives of the Great War period referred to the Yorkshire Regiment.

41st Division (to Western Front, Spring 1918)   WO95/4241
Divisional troops – Pioneers: 19/Middlesex   WO95/4242
122 Bde: 12/East Surrey, 15/Hampshire
    (Hampshire Carabineers), 11/R. West Kent,
    18/KRRC   WO95/4243
123 Brigade: 11/Queen's, 10/R. West Kent,
    23/Middlesex, 20/DLI   WO95/4243
124 Brigade: 10/Queen's, 26/Royal Fusiliers,
    32/RF, 21/KRRC   WO95/4243

Note on British, French and American operations in Italy.

The British and Frnch Expeditionary Forces arrived in Italy in late 1917. They were initially to be used as a backstop for the Italian Armies on the recently-established Piave Front, but in December 1917 were deployed into a critical corner of that front; the GOCs reported directly to the Italian C-in-C.

In March 1918 the two Expeditionary Forces were reduced from two to one Army Corps in order to send troops back to the Western Front to bolster the defences in the face of the imminent German offensive. The remaining corps were re-deployed to the Asiago Plateau, becoming part of Sixth (Italian)Army (GOC Luca Montuori).

In June 1918 the Sixth Army bore the brunt of a major Austrian offensive across the plateau, part of *Operation Radetzky*. The fortunes of the French are not well-recorded, and are only covered in the barest outline here, enough to give, it is hoped, some feel for the terrain in relation to the events of June 1918. The two Allied corps spent much of their time on the Asiago Plateau either labouring to improve the defences, or taking the war to the enemy in patrols and trench raids.

In July 1918 a US Expeditionary Force of one infantry regiment and support services arrived in Italy from France. It did not form part of any Allied formation until early September when one battalion was deployed onto the Piave Front, coming under tactical control of the Italian 37th Division.

Please note that this guide only covers some of the ground where the three contingents served between November 1917 and September 1918. It is intended to cover the complex assault crossing of the Piave, and the advances to the rivers Tagliamento (east of the Piave) and Fèrsina (north of the Asiago Plateau) in the future.

In October 1918 the two corps were reduced in size and re-deployed to the Piave Front as the nuclei of two new Allied formations; Tenth and Twelfth Armies. The former comprised XIV (Br) and XI (It) Corps under Lieutenant General The Earl of Cavan; each corps had two divisions; respectively the British 7th and 23rd, and the Italian 23rd and 37th – including the US 332nd Infantry Regiment and its support services. The Twelfth Army comprised I (It) and XI (Fr) Corps, with the 24th and 70th Italian, and the 23rd French and 52nd Italian Divisions; GOC was the French General Jean Cesar Graziani.

The British 48th (South Midland), and the French 24eme Divisions remained on the Asiago Plateau under tactical control of XI (It) Corps, Sixth Army. The Tenth and Twelfth Armies, and the Eighth (all Italian) Army, spearheaded the final thrust across the river Piave, between 23 October to 4 November 1918, when an Armistice took effect in the Italian theatre. The two Allied divisions on the Asiago Plateau joined Italian units in the final advance which took them well inside Austrian territory before the Armistice took effect.

The US contingent, through no fault of their own, did not experience combat until the closing hour or so of the campaign. After the Armistice all three national contingents sent troops to parts of the former Austro-Hungarian Empire, some by then in the new nation of Jugoslavia. British troops went to what are now Albania, Austria and Croatia; French soldiers to Austria and Croatia, and Americans to Albania, Austria, Croatia and Montenegro, at that time still – just – an independent state.

In 2002 British, French and American troops returned to Albania, Croatia, Bosnia and Kosovo, Yugoslavia.

Prelude

In May 1915 the Kingdom of Italy entered the Great War as one of the Entente nations. A few weeks later the Italian Army attacked the Austrian frontier defences and achieved some success, mainly in the mountains north of Trieste. Here the *Commando Supremo*, General Luigi Cadorna, orchestrated a series of desperate assaults known as the Battles of the Isonzo. In August 1917 the eleventh of these violent clashes left the Austrians in dire straits. The *k.u.k.* was generally in a bad way after three years of heavy losses in Russia, Serbia and Italy, and desperate for relief. The AOK turned to their German allies who came up with a plan for a short offensive to push the Italians out of the mountains. In late October 1917 the Battle of Caporetto not only pushed the Italians onto the plains but forced them back to the river Piave, where the CS managed to organise and establish a new front line. The despised Austro-Hungarians were back in the Veneto, this time accompanied by fit, battle-hardy and disciplined German divisions, and it was the turn of the Italians to seek help.

Early in the battle General Cadorna appealed to the French and British for assistance, on the basis of an inter-Allied agreement made in December 1915 during a conference at Chantilly, near Paris. Britain, France, Italy, Russia and Serbia had each undertaken to hold itself in readiness to stop any enemy offensive on its own front with its own resources, and to assist, to the fullest possible extent, an ally faced with a similar situation. A year later, at another conference, mutual support was again discussed, and talk changed to planning. The British and

Austrian-German advance from Caporetto, October-November 1917.

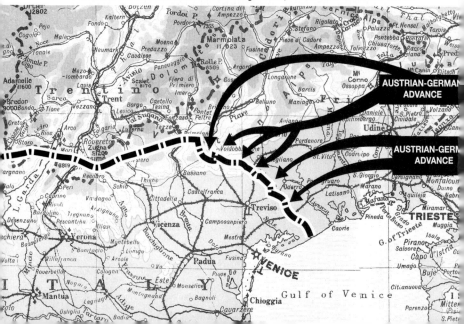

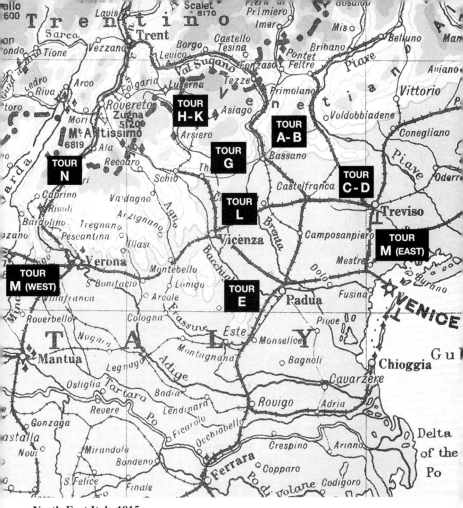

North-East Italy 1915

French each envisaged sending an expeditionary force of two Army corps; about 120,000 men and 26,000 horses, to Italy. The British plans were prepared under the direction of Brigadier General JHV Crowe, assisted in Italy by the British Military Mission, Italian staff officers and representatives of the British and Italian Foreign Offices. The Official History contains a good description of the plans and the associated administrative procedures. French staff officers in the *Théatres d'Opérations Extérieures* (TOE) section of the GQG and Italian officers in the CS made similar arrangements.

Thanks to the hard work of these officers, after Cadorna's appeal French and British troops were quickly sent to Italy. By 27 October French advance parties were in Italy and British teams followed a few

K.u.k. cooks and *gulaschekanone.* Roger Garbett collection

days later. Most military trains in France and Flanders were generally of a standard 'consist': engine, two coaches, thirty of the dreaded *Chevaux 8 Hommes 40 vans*, seventeen flat cars for vehicles and stores, and two brake vans. One train could carry any unit or sub-unit where the permutation of men and animals did not exceed the capacity of the box-vans; e.g. half an infantry battalion, or half an RFC

German troops in Italy after Caporetto

Chevaux 8 Hommes 40 type wagon (Horses 8 Men 40); British troops going home 1919. IWM Q25795

squadron. As the journey to Italy would take at least five days, space had to be found for rations and forage. As it was thought the troops might go straight into action so pick-axes, spades and sandbags also had to be crammed into the vans.

Most accounts of Great War journeys bemoan the slow speed of the trains. Throughout France, Flanders and Italy, military trains were scheduled to travel through each section of a route at a specific speed, which averaged 30 kph/17^1/$_2$ mph for every journey. This unhurried progress may have exasperated the troops, but it helped the railway authorities control, as much as war conditions allowed, complex traffic movements.

The journey may have been slow and uncomfortable, but it acted as a powerful tonic to the weary troops. Edward Corbett, the well-educated, much-travelled and overage Regimental Quartermaster Sergeant Major of 1/8 Worcesters wrote:

> *Dawn found us at Longueval, not far from Paris; next dawn we were beside the great Sâone in Beaujolais. The men were enraptured by the scenery. So down the long, lovely valley beneath the Cèvennes, and over the Isère, till evening time we saw the high snows of the Dauphiny [sic]... we seemed to be in a new continent – houses of a new type, olive and orange trees, cypresses and aloes, a bright sun, a buoyant sparkling air, white*

hard roads, ('fancy, a dry road, Alf'), and now those lovely bays.
The British Expeditionary Force (Italy) detrained around Mantua, south of Verona, and were briefly held in that area as a backstop in case the enemy onslaught crossed the Piave. The GOC was General Sir Henry Plumer, at that time commanding Second Army in France, and one of the best British commanders of the Great War. The fact that Field Marshal Sir Douglas Haig selected him to command the expeditionary force indicated the seriousness with which the British authorities viewed the threat to the Italian nation, the Otranto Barrage and the Mediterranean seaborne lines of communication.

British MP and Italian Carabinieri. Taylor Collection

Many British accounts dwell on the problems of unloading large numbers of men, animals and vehicles at small country stations with limited facilities. The situation was hindered by a lack of interpreters; each battalion was supposed to have one Italian Liaison Officer fluent in English and several interpreters. Even if one was available he might be Neapolitan and unable to understand the Mantovan stationmaster, and possibly speak English with a pronounced American accent. Corbett wrote about one of these interpreters:

> *Through a little town (Albaredo) we marched to a hamlet ... here Major Bate achieved a feat which added indescribably to our comfort and well-being all the time we were in Italy: he stole an interpreter, an Italian soldier from London, Luigi Ciapancelli by name, Lulu to our tongues and in our hearts, the best little man that ever made macaroni scarce.*

Fortunately many of the Carabinieri, who in Italy carried out many of the functions of military police, spoke some English. All were intelligent and energetic; having by force of circumstances to work closely with British MPs they soon became fluent, as did many of their English colleagues in Italian, to the surprise of their officers and countrymen.

Norman Gladden, a private soldier in 11/Northumberland Fusiliers, noted that the British were in Italy to set an example:

> *On our arrival in Italy we had been admonished to keep smart and emulate the Guards. During the preceding days much spit and polish had been expended. We were now expected to create an impression, to inspire confidence in the people, who were to see and hear about the Allied contingents marching with drums beating and fifes playing in smartly-uniformed and well-aligned columns of four, towards the field of battle.*

The local population, and newspaper reporters from across Italy, were

Monte Grappa. Southern face, showing the war road

suitably impressed by the long columns of Allied soldiers; smart, disciplined, healthy, cheerful and vigorous. They were in sharp contrast to stragglers from Caporetto slowly making their way westwards. These *Sbanditi* were shepherded into assembly areas well away from the operational zone; quiet places where shattered units could rally, and exhausted and demoralised men recover in body and soul. But the Italian nation rallied after the disaster at Caporetto; and propaganda posters appeared everywhere, exhorting everyone to fight and support the nation in its time of danger.

FRATELLI SALVATEMI!
SOTTOSCRIVETE !

Fratelli Salvatemi! Sottoscrivete!
Brothers, save us! Subscribe [buy war bonds]. FM

The French

The French expeditionary force, the Tenth Army (GOC General Duchêne), were concentrated west of Verona, around the southern shores of Lake Garda, partly to counter a rumoured Austro-German offensive down the valley of the river Adige from the Tyrol.

Some of the French troops knew they were marching in their forefathers' footsteps. The Tenth Army passed the battleground of Solferino where, in August 1859, a French army fought an Austrian one; both claimed a victory. The resulting carnage, or rather the sufferings of the wounded left where they fell in the full heat of summer, eventually led to the formation of the International Red Cross. Some French officers knew about the Battle of the Piava (correct spelling at that time, May 1809), when a Napoleonic Franco-Italian Army waded the river near Nervesa and defeated an Austrian army retreating from the Veneto; in 1917 the tale was recounted in cafés and considered to be a good omen.

The Piave Front

By mid-November the Italians were esconced in a new front line along the west bank of the Piave. The river left the mountains at the east end of the Monte Grappa *massif,* which dominates two strategic routes onto the Venetian plain; the Brenta and Piave valleys. In November 1917 the

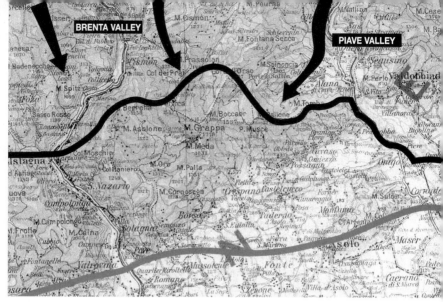

Grappa massif: Threats to the Brenta and Piave valleys, and the Piave front line, November-December 1917.

upper reaches of both were firmly in the hands of the enemy. In the west an Austrian offensive on the Asiago Plateau had pushed the Italian front line back towards the escarpment above Bassano del Grappa at the mouth of the Brenta valley. Any further advance would unmask the Italian defences on the western flank of Grappa, and expose the vital supply links – war roads, mule tracks, cableways – running up the southern face. If the Italians lost control of the west flank of Grappa the Brenta valley would be open to an enemy offensive into the allied rear areas.

Grappa was also threatened from the east, by enemy forces thrusting down the Piave valley from the Dolomites. Austrian and German troops had penetrated down the side of the *massif* and attempted to storm the eastern flank and push the Italians off the summit. They were unsuccessful, but by 25 November had established a small but important salient on Monte Tomba, a summit on the Monfenera ridge on the eastern flank of Grappa. Monfenera is the most southerly high ridge of the mountains backing the Venetian plain, and it overlooked the Italian defences along the Piave and the Italian supply and administrative areas in Montebelluna and Treviso. If this salient was exploited the new Italian defences on the eastern flank of Grappa and along the Piave would be out-flanked. And as many Italian units were still shaken by recent events there might have been another 'Caporetto'. So the north-east corner of the new Italian front line was critically important, and had to be held at all costs.

The Italians had a new CS, General Armando Diaz. He was convinced the enemy forces were capable of continuing their offensive, and of forcing his troops off Grappa and outflanking the Piave line. He discussed the situation at length with Generals Plumer and Duchêne, who stated that, provided the Italians did not panic in the face of persistent enemy attacks, the front line could be held by the forces then to hand, and some months of work would make it almost impregnable. They also discussed the role of their expeditionary forces as it was reported that some Italian units along the Piave, shaken by events in the east, had been told that all they had to do was hold out until the Allies arrived to relieve them. The Allied generals made it clear that in accordance with the Chantilly agreements the expeditionary forces were there to help, not bear the brunt of the fighting. But they agreed it would be impolitic for their troops to be seen loitering in the rear, so a sensible compromise was reached. The British and French would deploy one each corps into the front line, in the critical sector east of Grappa. The other Allied corps would be held in depth as part of a multi-national counter-attack force.

General (later Field-Marshal Armando Diaz, Commando Supremo, 1917-1924 wearing insignia of the US Distinguished Service Cross.

Piave Front: Allied concentration areas and lines of advance. November 1917.

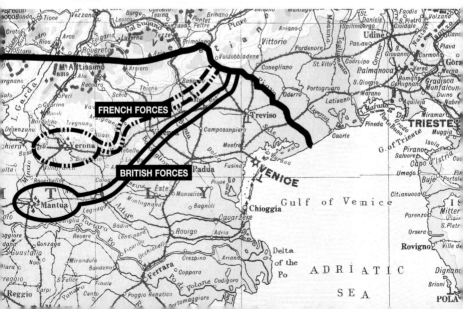

THE PIAVE FRONT

TOUR A
Monte Tomba and Monfenera
December 1917 – March 1918

Introduction

The Monte Tomba – Monfenera ridge is a 2,000 foot-high hog's back running eastwards from the Grappa *massif* for about six kilometres to end abruptly at the Piave. It is flanked by shallow basins, each drained by a small river; the Ornic to the north and the Ponticello to the south. In late 1917 the slopes running down to these basins were covered with rough pastures and scattered woods, crossed by a few cow tracks. The ridge and basins are pleasant in summer, but Monfenera is desolate in autumn, and a wilderness in winter, and in 1917 the tracks leading up from the basins were useless for moving troops, supplies and heavy weapons.

The ridge looks innocuous, but it was the key to Grappa and the Piave river line. The eastern end covered the road and the railway from Feltre, the only routes on the west bank of the Piave river by which guns and supplies could be brought forward to support an enemy breakthrough round or over Grappa. The ridge also provided excellent observation over much of the Piave defences and it could also be used as a bridge for attacks against the inadequate Italian defences on the

The Allied North Piave Line, winter 1917-1918: French sectors (M. Tomba-Pederobba), Italian sector (Covolo), British (Montello-Arcade) sectors.

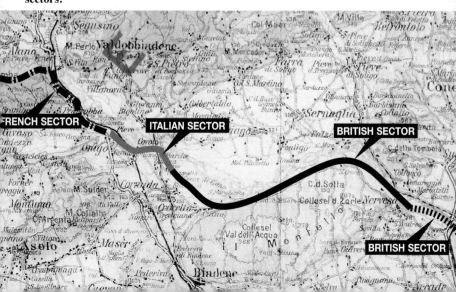

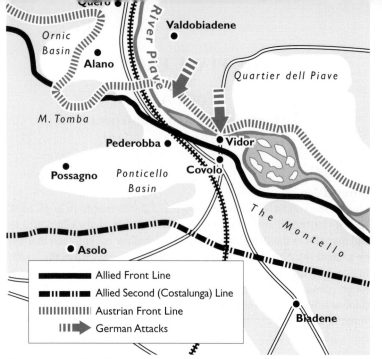

Quero

Valdobiadene

River Piave

Ornic Basin

Alano

Quartier dell Piave

M. Tomba

Pederobba

Vidor

Possagno

Ponticello Basin

Covolo

Asolo

The Montello

Biadene

Allied Front Line

Allied Second (Costalunga) Line

Austrian Front Line

German Attacks

Piave Front: The Monte Tomba-Monfenera Ridge area of operations, December 1917.

south-eastern shoulder of Grappa. Monfenera was critically important to both sides, and Monte Tomba, looming above the main ridge, was the key to its security.

The enemy salient overlooked a new Italian front line, originally a shallow reserve trench about three hundred metres down the southern side of the ridge. The salient gave the enemy excellent observation across the Ponticello basin to a line of low hills, the *Colli Àsolani*. But the ground on either side of the salient was held by Italian troops, and

View from the west end of the M. Tomba-Monfenera Ridge across the Possagno basin to the Colli Àsolani, Montello and the Piave.

QUARTIER DEL PIAVE

PIAVE

THE MONTEL

COLLI ÀSOLANI

PONTICELLO BASIN

POSSAGN

Impressed civilians working on a communication trench between the Italians and the Austrians near Àsolo. <small>Museo della Grande Guerra, Canove</small>

they in turn had excellent views over the Ornic basin and of the village of Alano di Piave, through which every and track from the ridge seemed to pass. To the west of the basin more Italian OPs, in telephone contact with machine-gun posts and artillery batteries, covered the slopes up which enemy reinforcements and supply columns had to travel. At night the basin was swept by Italian searchlights, and any movement caught in their beams attracted instant accurate gunfire. Conversely, the Italians had little trouble maintaining their positions on the ridge. Supplies and reinforcements passed along the trenches from the main Grappa line, or up from the Piave valley; laborious, but relatively safe. The Italians made little use of the slopes leading up to Monfenera, but the basin held a peculiar complication for them, and a moral dilemma for some Austrians. Below M. Tomba lies the small town of Possagno and the *Tempio Canoviano*, the Temple of Canova. This is a world-famous church, gifted to his home town in 1819 by the sculptor Antonio Canova, and its magnificent white cupola can be seen for miles. The Temple survived the war – just, but that story must be told elsewhere. (There are rumours of a local truce after the Germans left, and of the intercession of Empress Zita of Austria.)

Costalunga Line

The *Colli Àsolani* was the site of a large secondary defence line to the south of the front line. The *Colli Àsolani* section was referred to as the Costalunga Line by the British, who built much of it, and of the next section which bisected the Montello and ended at the river Piave near the shattered town of Nervesa. The line was a key component in the defences of the critical corner between the Piave and the mountain defence lines, and as long as the enemy held onto the salient they could direct artillery fire onto the line and its attendant working parties from gun positions near Valdobiadene.

Life in the salient was difficult; the top of the ridge is a barren, windswept place at the best of times, and the winter of 1917/18 was severe. The garrison huddled in makeshift trenches and dugouts, which they could only develop slowly as food and ammunition had priority over tools and defence stores for carrying parties from Alano. Food was scarce, drinking water scarcer still, warmth almost unknown and sleep near impossible as the Italians sniped, machine-gunned and bombarded the salient and its defenders at every opportunity. And if that was not bad enough, by mid-December winter had arrived in full force. Blizzards, gales and sub-zero temperatures made life almost unbearable even for the fittest soldier; the fate of the injured and sick can be imagined. The salient served no useful purpose; it was a steady drain on scarce resources and in reality could never be used as a sally-port into the Grappa and Piave defences. But the *k.u.k.* obstinately refused to accept that, and insisted it remain occupied. And the *CS* saw it as a real threat, and wanted something done about it – quickly.

Monfenera: rough open ground; looking north across the Alano basin.

Clearing the Salient

The Italians did not have mountain troops, *Alpini*, available and the British had neither experience nor training in mountain warfare, but the French had studied and practised it for years in the Alps. They also had recent mountain fighting experience of a sort in the Vosges, and had sensibly added two divisions of *Chasseurs Alpins* to Tenth Army, so were the only choice for clearing the salient.

The French deployed XXXI Corps into the Monfenera sector, its two divisions, the 64th and 65th,

Chasseurs Alpins: 65mm Mountain gun.

augmented by the 47th *Chasseurs Alpin* Division, and an Italian *Alpini* brigade. The 47th Division occupied the Monfenera ridge and the 65th the river line, with the *Alpini* guarding a particularly sensitive location, the exits from a partly demolished bridge over the Piave. The 64th Division was in depth around Bassano del Grappa, and the Corps troops were on the Venetian plain south-west of Àsolo. XII (Fr) Corps remained west of Vicenza as part of the multi-national counter-attack force mentioned earlier.

On 3 December advance parties from XXXI Corps started taking over the sector from the Italians, and the Chasseurs immediately set about preparing to clear the salient. Much of the reconnaissance and planning was carried out by a Colonel Bel, of the *Chasseurs Alpins*. Accompanied by artillery and engineer officers and a small escort he surveyed the southern face of the ridge, selecting approach routes and assembly areas. The team also examined the Austrian defences in great detail, and at close quarters. The *k.u.k.* defenders took exception to this, and sent strong patrols outside their wire to attack or ambush the recce parties. On 13 December they also mounted local attacks at both ends of the salient, supported by German batteries about to depart for the Western Front; they fired off all their ammunition as it could not be moved to France. The attacks failed to disturb the French, but a rumour that their line had broken somehow travelled into the rear areas. The British 7th Division, recently arrived in a reserve position some 20 kilometres to the south was stood to arms, but not required. (Which was perhaps just as well; the Division had recently received reinforcements, many barely trained and not yet battle-fit, and the thought of attempting to deploy them into the hills to tackle a break-out by Austrian mountain troops must have given General Plumer some anxious moments.)

Meanwhile, along the river line the 65th Division strengthened the improvised barricades across the road and railway and improved the trenches and dug-outs. They also conducted aggressive 'reconnaissance by fire' of likely enemy locations in the surrounding hills, and tried to get patrols across the Piave to probe the enemy defences. But the river was turbulent and fast, and no report of a successful crossing has been located. In any case there was little to find on the east bank, apart from some wire and a few outposts. The Germans were withdrawing from Italy, and the Austrians busy establishing themselves in abandoned towns and villages before winter had arrived in force.

On 24 December 1917 the Austrian high command issued a triumphant bulletin announcing the capture of the first French prisoner of war on the Italian Front: there was less to crow about a few days later. The French assault was supported by massed artillery working to a meticulously-planned programme. The organic corps and divisional assets (144 guns) was supplemented by forty batteries of French, Italian and British field, mountain and heavy artillery, producing around 450 guns, to support the assault and interdict enemy counter-attacks. The movement and siting of the guns, allocation of targets, calculation of ammunition requirements and planning of fire missions was under the direct supervision of General Liset, the senior artillery officer in Tenth Army. He was a highly decorated veteran of Verdun, and much of the success of the attack on Monte Tomba was due to his meticulous planning and inspired leadership of artillerymen of three nations. (He was killed early in April 1918 during a German air raid on Castelfranco Veneto, site of the GQG.)

On 30 December 1917 the assault commenced with a five hour artillery barrage, by what appeared to one observer to be every gun in Italy. At 2 pm three battalions of *Chasseurs Alpins*, the 51st (right flank), 115th (centre), and 70th (left flank), started to leave their assembly areas below the salient, followed by regimental pioneers laden with defence stores. The assault force quickly advanced through an enemy defensive barrage and stormed the trenches where the Austrians were overwhelmed within thirty minutes. It was a brilliant example of a carefully planned and executed set-piece attack, with perfect co-ordination between the artillery and infantry. The enemy lost 500 dead, 1,500 captured and lost many machine-guns, mortars and light field guns. The French sustained some 250 casualties, including fifty-four dead. Among the first to fall was Colonel Bel, described by the Italians as 'robust and courageous' (*aitante e valoroso*).

The Austrians withdrew from much of the Ornic basin, leaving a few outposts around Alano, and light defences on the slopes to the north, opposite Monfenera. The *k.u.k.* retained forces in the river valley area: a small supply base and an artillery HQ were set up in Quero, as well as a field hospital. A German-built artillery OP was used to watch the French road block near Pederobba, and British forces on the Montello.

TOUR ROUTE A:
Possagno, Monfenera, Alano, Quero
Start: A4/A31 junction.
Maps: LAC Vicenza, Treviso

Accommodation: There are several good hotels in and around Montebelluna, catering mainly for business people as it is a busy industrial centre; the world HQ of Bennenton is just down the road, for example. On the Montello the *Albergo alla Pinetta* above Biadene is quiet and comfortable. It also has several single rooms in addition to the usual twin/doubles, (and some triples). The food in the adjacent restaurant is excellent and inexpensive. And the owner has his own vineyard (*www.sevenonline/allapineta*)

Suggested reading: *Rommel and Caporetto*; Chapter Nine.

Caution: The ridge is very popular in summer, especially at weekends when the approach roads and summit area can be very busy. It is a mecca for mountain bikers, so keep a sharp look-out if walking on paths away from the road.

Itinerary: From the A4/A31 junction take the **A31** and drive north (towards the mountain wall) to the first exit and take the **SS53** eastbound for Cittadella. Drive past Cittadella and Castelfranco Veneto and take the **SS667** for Montebelluna/Feltre. Drive for 17 kms to a large roundabout, near Caerano di San Marco. Take the second exit, ie straight on, for Feltre. After about 4 kms the **SS667** merges with the **SS348** for *Feltre*, and 5 kms further on follow the signs for *Possagno* via a slip-road and clover-leaf junction. (Ignore for the moment the French War Memorial on the left; it is difficult to reach from the northbound lane and is described below.)

Drive to *Possagno*. The Temple of Canova is well worth a visit, if only to use the carpark as a vantage point to study the slopes of Monfenera and the *Colli Àsolani*. From Possagno go east past **Cavaso del Tomba**; for the road for **Alano di Piave/Monte Tomba**. Turn left up that road and at the top park near Monte Tomba – which is unmistakable, and has numerous paths up to the summit. The French attacked (roughly) across the whole of the summit area, an amazing feat of arms which deserves closer study. The views are striking, especially to the north over the Ornic basin and Alano, and south and east across the lower Piave. A look over the north edge of the ridge into the Ornic basin, and then back to the view south to the *Colli Àsolani* brings into focus the problems of supply. Look east to Valdobiadene and then south-east to the flat ground opposite the Montello to understand the value of the ridge as an Allied OP.

Return to the car and take the road downhill to **Alano di Piave**. This is a quiet little village; and a good place to study the surrounding slopes. Those to the west and north twice saw bitter fighting; in November 1917, when Austrian and German forces attempted to seize the summits, then in October 1918 when Italian troops advanced north from Grappa and Monfenera at the start of the Battle of Vittorio Veneto.

There is a small museum in Alano, the *Museo Storica della Guerra 1915-1918*, in the Via Marconi, open only on Sundays, but with some interesting items and information on the life and times of the village and its inhabitants during the Great War years.

The next stop is **Quero**, site of a **German War Memorial.**

Quero

Drive out of Alano towards the east and take the first right, then turn left at the T-junction onto the road for **Quero**. Drive to the village square; on the east (valley) side is a yellow sign for the **Deutscher Soldatenfriedhof**. Drive down the **Via Giovanni XXIII** and after about 1.5 kms start looking right for the entrance to the (small) cemetery car park. The custodian's house is on the left of the entrance to the car-park. On the right of the house is an archway marking the start of the

German Cemetery, Quero. Mauro Agostinetti

path to the memorial. Just inside the archway is a small display of postcards and information leaflets, including English language ones, and a visitors' book. A short walk across an orchard takes visitors to the rear of the memorial, which is built on the Col Maor, a gentle slope above the Piave gorge.

The building houses a mass grave and a memorial. It was built on the site of the German artillery OP (Post B) mentioned earlier, and has excellent views down the river valley, and of the slopes where many of the German and Austrian soldiers buried here died. The memorial was built between 1936 and 1939 under the direction of an Austrian architect, Otto Mayr, of Innsbruck. The design, also used for another memorial at Pordoi in the Trentino Region, is supposedly derived from that of Inca forts. Be that as it may, the buildings are solid, well made and impressive, and in harmony with the mountain settings. The remains of 229 German soldiers from the Alpine Corps, and 3,232 Austrian soldiers from many regiments and nationalities, are encased in an external wing of the building; the gate protecting the sepulchre is made of gun barrels welded together. Inside the memorial there is a *Gedenkraum* (Commemoration Room). This is on the left of the entrance, beyond three archways. In the centre of the rather dark Gedenkraum is a stone altar made from a single slab of black Swedish granite. It supports metal-paged books containing the names and places of origin of the 865 identifiable bodies. The plinth is illuminated by a skylight, the room's only source of light; in high summer it loses some of its sombre Wagnerian atmosphere. Running round the top of the walls is a frieze depicting, in bas-relief, twelve German soldiers. Beneath the frieze is an inscription:

> *Wir standen zusammen in Reih und Glied wir standen zusammen im Leben*
> *Drum gleiches Kreuz und gleicher Schmuck ward uns aufs Grab gegeben.*
> *Nun ruhen wir aus vom heissen Streit und harren getrost der Ewigkeit*

> *We stood together in the ranks and we stood together in life.*

French Memorial, Pederobba. FM

*Therefore the same cross and same honour were bestowed on
our tomb. Now we can rest from the fiery battle and wait
consoled for eternity.*

This memorial is very different from British, Commonwealth or
American ones, but is a handsome and dignified tribute to the dead
soldiers, and was placed in a fine and not inappropriate setting. The
memorial is beautifully maintained, and a sombre reminder of the
human cost of war; it is not as well known or visited as it deserves.

It is maintained by the VDK, the *Volksbund Deutsche
Kriegsgräberfürsorge*, the German equivalent of the CWGC. The
VDK maintains eight memorials in northern Italy (and one in Slovenia,
at Tolmin, near Caporetto; Karfreit to the Germans, Kobarid to the
Slovenes). Six Italian sites commemorate 16,380 German dead from
the Great War: Bolzano, Bressanone, Brunico, Feltre, Pordoi and
Quero. The Tolmin memorial commemorates 946 German soldiers.

There is no Austrian equivalent of the VDK. After the Great War the
government of the new-born Austrian Republic had neither the will nor
the wherewithal to commemorate the dead of the defunct *k.u.k.* Many
of the dead were from newly independent nations who did not want any
Austrian involvement in their affairs and had more pressing matters to
deal with than the remains of dead soldiers in foreign lands. In the late
1930s Germany assumed responsibility for commemorating the *k.u.k.*
war dead in countries where such activity was tolerated.

The next tour follows on from this one, and includes the French War
Memorial south of Pederobba

Tour B
Pederobba and Vidor
Map: LAC Treviso

Itinerary: Return to the centre of Quero, and drive back the way you
came, heading for Fener and the **SS348**. The junction in Fener can be
interesting at times (particularly Sunday evenings in summer) with fast
traffic coming down from the left, heading home from a day-out in

Piave near Pederobba, 1998. FM

British and Italian troops building a road block and machine-gun position near Nogare, south of Covolo, winter, 1917. Taylor Collection

Feltre, Belluno or the Dolomites. Drive down the **SS348** and after 5 kms start looking right for the French War Memorial. It is unmistakable. (It lies south-east, and outside of Pederobba, a pleasant little town.)

Parking is tricky as there is only a small space next to the entrance pathway. The memorial consists of a huge concrete wall, faced with a thousand panels, one for each of the dead. Seated in front of the wall are the figures of a man and a woman, holding the corpse of a youth across their laps, and gazing mutely towards the east. The memorial overlooks part of the line held by the French in the winter of 1917/18, and is close to the eastern end of the Monte Tomba – Monfenera ridge. It also overlooks the sites of bridgeheads established in late October 1918 by French and Italian soldiers at the start of the Battle of Vittorio Veneto. The memorial commemorates all French soldiers killed in action or who died of wounds, accident or disease, and those listed as missing, in the Italian campaign. After the Great War considerable efforts were made to have the bodies disinterred and returned to France, but there is at least one intriguing anomaly, described in Tour L.

The bridge between Vidor (right) and Covolo. IWM Q26280

Further back along the road from Fener on the opposite side of the **SS348** in a lay-by near Pederobba railway station, where there is a plaque commemorating the crossing of the Piave in October 1918, and the role played by the French in the Battle of Vittorio Veneto. The plaque is a few minutes walk along road; beware speeding traffic. While on that side of the road it is possible to gain an idea of the problems facing French troops along the river line in the winter of 1917/18. The front line trenches were very close to the water, and in full view of Austrian OPs on the hills above Valdobiadene, and well within range of artillery hidden in the folds and hollows of the slopes. The role of the French troops in this part of the line was dangerous and thankless, but for three winter months their vigilance and artillery made sure that the Austrians had little rest, and few chances of getting patrols across the river. Near Pederobba the Piave is relatively narrow and could be approached under cover of woods and vineyards along the hills behind Valdobiadene on the eastern bank. Valdobiadene itself could be reached by a road running up the valley of the Soligo from the railway at Vittorio Veneto, a name later to become famous. The line had been demolished in places by Italian rearguards, but the *k.u.k.* had three years experience of repairing railways in Russia and Serbia, and had just acquired large quantities of Italian track and rolling stock.

The next stop is *Covolo*, where an Italian garrison, under French command, covered a bridge vital to both sides and almost intact. Rejoin the **SS348** southbound, and immediately look for a sign for **Levada**. Take that road, and find your way from there to **Covolo**, at the southern end of a road bridge leading to Vidor and Valdobiadene.

The bridge at Vidor
In November 1917 this bridge was a major concern to the Allies, hence the brigade-sized covering force. The bridge was a sturdy, stone built structure spanning the Piave at a particularly narrow point, where it

MONFENERA RIDGE   QUERO-FENER GAP

Italian-built front line trenches along the banks of the Piave; Barche, 1918. IWM Q 26280

passed between two outcrops of rock. It was approached from the north by two good roads running along one of these outcrops and therefore above the frequent floods. On 10 November the enemy nearly captured the bridge intact when an advance guard from the German 12th Division surprised the small Italian covering force in Vidor and raced across the bridge for the south bank. They were stopped by intense machine-gun fire and withdrew into Vidor. That night Italian engineers demolished three of the spans, and cratered others. The piers were almost indestructible; it was, and still is, very robust. Next day the Germans made another attempt to cross the river using the damaged bridge and wading the river alongside, but were stopped before making any serious headway. A substantial part of the bridge remained intact, and the CS knew that it represented a major threat. But it was also going to be needed, someday, for a counter-attack to expel the Austrians from the Veneto, so had to be retained more or less intact,

Piave river bed, from the Covolo - Vidor bridge, showing where German troops attempted to cross the river. 11 Novemeber 1918. FM

VALDOBIADENE RIDGE

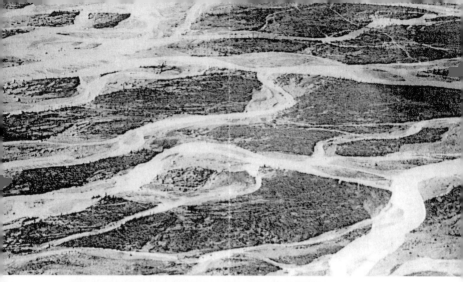

Piave bed, showing channels and *grave*, June 1918. Worcestershire Regt

but with the exits covered by strong defences. Hence the Costalunga Line, and the massed Allied artillery covering Monfenera, the bridge, and the exits from it to the south.

The road to the bridge is usually busy, so park wherever you can once it comes into view. A café car park is useful, for even questions in elementary Italian may produce a speaker of English, or of American, and a lot of information about the village and the bridge during the *Grande Guerra*. It may even produce a guided tour of the river bank, where there are remains of machine-gun posts, admittedly under about six feet of prickly undergrowth.

Once the situation stabilized on 11 November 1917 the *Alpini* started to strengthen the trenches and dugouts along the river bank and, helped by British troops, erected road blocks and machine-gun posts covering the roads leading away from the bridge. Downstream, in the village of Barche, machine-gun posts were built in the foundations of houses on the water's edge, next to trenches on the top of the bank. Some of the embrasures can still be seen in winter, but the posts and their access tunnels have long been filled in to maintain the integrity of the embankments in times of flood.

That is the last stop in this tour. The next one deals with the British in the Montello and Arcade sectors, so either return to the Caerano roundabout – turning across the traffic close to the bridge can be interesting – or continue along the **SS348** over the bridge to visit Vidor and Valdobiadene, famous for its wines. Then for the Montello Tour, head south following signs for Cornuda, rejoin the **SS348** and drive to the Caerano roundabout.

TOUR C
The Montello
December 1917 – March 1918

Introduction

The Piave was outside the experience of most of the British and French military engineers. It was fast (up to 14 mph at times), wide, cold, turbulent and subject to sudden floods. It rises high in the Dolomites, close to the Austrian frontier, and winds through the mountains for some hundred miles before reaching the Venetian plain. The river therefore has an enormous upland catchment area which is subject to heavy rain and snow dumped by moist Adriatic winds. From Fener to the Adriatic the river bed is flanked by *bunds*. Wherever the river crosses flat land the frequent floods scour exposed an ever-changing pattern of channels and runnels and the shingle. Shingle beds which survive for any length of time soon acquire a coating of vegetation making them even more resistant to all but the worst floods; these are *grave*, some of the larger ones qualified by name, either from the location, such as *Grave di Ciano*, or alternatively, of the owner, as in *Grave di Papadopoli*, named after a Venetian family of Greek extraction.

Below Vidor the river skirts a small plain, the *Quartier del Piave,* where at one point in 1917 the river bed was over three kilometres wide, and laced with dozens of runnels and channels. Some channels were up to six feet deep, and ran between steep-sided shingle banks and around a large island, the *Grave di Ciano*. Below the *grave* the river is deflected by the bulk of a long hill, the Montello, and curls along its base before passing through a defile above the town of

Damaged road and railway bridges between Susegana and Ponte Priùla.
Worcestershire Regt

The Montello, winter 1917/18; note ferry boat symbols at Falzè and Nervesa and the absence of Strada Dorsale and the limited number of *prese*.

Nervesa. It then entered a stretch of *grave* and shingle beds, before narrowing at Borgo di Molino, a tiny village on the eastern bank. It then runs across a vast area of reclaimed swamp to the sea.

There were road or rail bridges at Fener, Vidor, and between Susegana Station and Ponte Priùla, near Nervesa, as well as some small passenger ferries and fords; but the retreating Italians rendered the bridges unusable, removed the ferry boats and wrecked the approaches and beds of the fords.

In 1809 General Macdonald (a Frenchman of Scots descent) described the Piave *as a wide and swift torrent, like all those in Italy; but they can all be forded except in the case of heavy rain or melting snow.* This was correct for an army of the Napoleonic era, but a Great War army depended on lorries, which required bridges, and even improvised bridges required untrammeled possession of foreshores, islands and bridgeheads.

The Montello, winter 1917/18. British patrol crossing sites.

Dolini on the Montello. FM

The German and Austrian armies had experience of bridging fast mountain rivers in the Carpathians and Transylvanian Alps, and were equipped with good, robust pontoons and bridging equipment. But, the small amount of bridging equipment deployed for the Caporetto offensive had been used to replace bridges demolished by the withdrawing Italians and would not be available for some time. However the Italians did not know that; they only knew the enemy had hustled them from the Isonzo to the Piave, crossing rivers with apparent ease, and that between Fener and Borgo there were too many good bridging sites for comfort.

A long stretch of the Piave is overlooked by the Montello, an isolated whale-backed hill, eight miles long by four wide, and 1,200 feet at its highest point. It dominates a large area of the Venetian plain, all of the *Quartier del Piave* and the eastern approaches to the *Colli Àsolani*. It forms a perfect observation platform and bastion at the

Italian troops testing barbed wire barriers at the edge of the Piave by the Montello. IWM Q 26280

point where the Piave is most easily crossed by an invading force so, in late 1917 whoever held the Montello controlled the eastern part of the front line.

The hill is glacial in origin and consists of a thick layer of soil over a bed of rock. The surface is dotted with deep hollows, *dolini,* caused by glacial action. Some are 300 feet across and sixty deep, and made excellent gun positions and bivouac areas. In 1917 the hill was thickly wooded; in mediaeval times it supplied timber for the piles on which Venice is built, and for the Serene Republic's shipyards.

The hill is encircled by roads, and crossed north-south by twenty-one numbered and named tracks [*prese* (sing. *Presa*) in the local dialect], originally forest lanes. Centuries of timber hauling has worn the *prese* deep into the steep hillside, ideal for removing tree trunks, not for the passage of heavy artillery. The Italian sappers built a longitudinal road with gentle gradients, the *Strada Dorsale*, which made life easier for the gun teams, and also speeded construction of an extension to the Costalunga Line.

A small town, Biadene, lies between the Montello and a long wooded hill, Pederiva Ridge on British war maps, formed by the Piave in ancient times when it ran south of the Montello. Beyond the ridge lies Montebelluna, in 1917 almost a ghost town.

Defences

As the Italian armies started to retreat from Caporetto, the CS hurriedly started making contingency plans for defence lines along the Piave and as far west as the river Mincio and Verona (that bald statement greatly oversimplifies a complex and rapidly-evolving situation) furthermore a scratch force of infantry and engineers rapidly fortified the Montello. They erected barbed wire barriers along the bed of the Piave and on the bank. Trenches were dug along the bank and this new front line followed a wavering course

Piave trenches. Worcestershire Regiment

Susegana; the demolished road and rail bridges used by German assault parties. As photographed in 1919. IWM Q 26181

from Fener to the Adriatic. It was built in a hurry, and lack of space along the river bank meant it was built without proper traverses: that and the soft soil meant it would not have survived an intense artillery barrage. Given the Italians' tactic of manning the front line with a mass of riflemen and machine-guns these riverside trenches would have been death-traps.

The front line was supported by two parallel lines of trenches, linked by deep communication trenches. There were rudimentary wire barriers between the lines, and a few simple switches. The front line had machine-gun posts at the head of T-shaped sprigs running forward from the main trench; mortar pits and ammunition bays were formed by similar sprigs running to the rear. Dugouts were burrowed into the back of the trench but offered no protection from shell-fire as they were only covered by a thin layer of logs and compacted soil; the best the harassed Italians could do in the time available. Once the enemy arrived at the Piave, work on the defences was frequently interrupted as troops stood to arms when there were attempts to cross the river. Apart from the attacks at Vidor and Valdobiadene mentioned above, on 13 November four battalions of the German 117th Division attempted to cross the river using rafts, boats and the piers of the ruined road and railway bridges between Susegana and Ponte Priùla. The Germans were repelled by heavy machine-gun fire, and many were killed or wounded. The few who reached the west bank became entangled in barbed wire and were killed or captured. Later that day Austrian troops occupied the *Grave di Papadopoli*, near the west bank of the river, but were also unable to advance any further in the face of fierce machine-gun fire.

Whilst none of the enemy attacks were successful, they diverted many Italians on the Montello away from their field engineering work. The Italian defenders needed respite, and the British arrived to take over the sector.

British Forces

On 30 November advance parties from XIV (Br) Corps started relieving I (It) Corps in the Montello sector; the take-over was complete by 4 December. The sector extended for about twenty kilometres from Crocetta to Nervesa. On the left was the *Alpini* Brigade of XXXI (Fr) Corps: the inter-corps boundary ran from Covolo to Crocetta, then to Nogare and Caerano di San Marco. The right inter-corps boundary ran from Nervesa almost due south towards Treviso. On

General Cavan in the Villa Emo, Fanzolo. IWM Q26622

Villa Emo, Fanzolo; XIV Corps HQ 1918. Emo family

the right flank of the British, in the Arcade sector, was VIII (It) Corps, part of the Italian Third Army, which was responsible for the Piave front from Nervesa to the Adriatic. In January 1918 XI (Br) Corps relieved VIII (It) Corps in the Arcade sector, but did not pass into Third Army, remaining part of the BEF(I).

The Montello sector was divided into the Ciano and Nervesa divisional sectors; each division had two brigades forward, and one in reserve. The inter-divisional boundary ran southwards from the water's edge opposite the north end of *Presa* 12. In the Ciano sector the left brigade sub-sector extended for 1,500 yards from Crocetta to *Presa* 18, and the right sector for nearly 5,000 yards from there to *Presa* 12. The Nervesa divisional sector started at *Presa* 12, the inter-brigade boundary was opposite the end of *Presa* 5, and the sector ended at the southern edge of Nervesa; each brigade sub-sector front was about 5,000 yards long.

On the extreme left the forward brigade had a short frontage as it was responsible for covering the area between the exit from the Vidor bridge and the hill. The extreme right brigade was responsible for two potential crossing points, the ferry and ford sites below San Croce and leading to Falzé di Piave, and at Nervesa. The rest of its front was along cliffs assumed to be impassable to attackers encumbered with artillery. (That was to be disproved by the *k.u.k.* in June 1918.)

Divisional HQs were established, after some shuffling around as accommodation was scarce, in Montebelluna and Volpago: not; Corps HQ was in the Villa Emo, at Fanzolo, southwest of Montebelluna, close to the French GQG in Castelfranco and the CS in Padua.

Occupation

The experiences of 23rd Division (General Sir James Babington) in the Ciano sector during winter 1917/18 were typical of the Corps' experience. The British took over Italian trench stores which included barrels of wine, much to the delight of the incoming soldiery. History does not record the fate of the wine, but the barrels were put to good use, as will be described later.

The Division immediately set about improving the defences. The wire at the water's edge required constant attention due to the force of the water; keeping it in good repair was a thankless task on a cold winter night, although fortunately the enemy lines were too far away for harassing machine-gun fire or trench mortar strafes.

The trenches were found to be only partly revetted, and then only with a single layer of woven bands of saplings, not sand bags. Machine gun posts were often in pulpit-like posts made from boulders cleverly cemented together, but lacking camouflage and overhead cover. They appeared vulnerable and obtrusive to the first British troops into the line, who decided to dig machine-gun posts into the *bund*. The first attempts to burrow into it, and to pierce the outer stone-faced walls, were immediately stopped by agitated Italian liaison officers. They

View from the Montello over critical exits from the Vidor-Covolo bridge.
Taylor Collection

British dug-outs under construction, west end of the Montello, M. Grappa in background. IWM Q 26114

warned that the force of a Piave flood would rip a breach and force the *bund* apart in minutes, and the waters would then scour the embankment, the ground behind and all the defences downstream. Thereafter the *bund* was left in peace; and the ubiquitous sand bag brought into use.

The British developed a rudimentary system of defence in depth, based on the existing front line trench. Listening posts were established along the water's edge, by the wire apron. At first these were close to the near bank, but were soon moved to shingle beds beyond the nearest channel. They were reached by light footbridges made from wire, stakes and corrugated iron. 'Listening' was a misnomer as near a Piave channel the rush and tumble of water over shingle made it difficult to hear a colleague shout even a few feet away. This was partly compensated for by the clarity of the air on frosty nights when, from the bank, movement against shingle beds could be seen a couple of hundred metres away by observers with binoculars, and sometimes by very sharp sighted, and alert, sentries. None of these posts were exactly

Captain Hardie, War Artist, photographed in late 1918, sketching for the painting *British Trenches on the edge of the Montello,* **overlooking the Piave.** IWM Q 26175

comfortable, and sentries had to be relieved frequently to prevent frost-bite or exposure.

Further east, from Ciano to Nervesa, the front line was realigned to take it above the river bed. New trenches were dug on the bank, incorporating Lewis gun posts sited to enfilade the river bed. These posts were lightly manned during the day but reinforced at night, and the main trenches covered by random patrols. The Italian second and third lines were strengthened when time allowed. New trench lines and Lewis gun posts were dug on the slopes of the Montello, covering the shelf between the river and the foot of the hill. The posts also covered the upper face of the hill along which ran another new line of trenches and posts.

In the left brigade sector the front line ran across flat land, where the gravelly soil was easy to work but useless for dug-outs. On 4 December the river rose and flooded the trenches, so the front line had to be re-located on higher ground and Italian engineers helped the British strengthen the trench sides and dug-outs with concrete and corrugated iron.

The ground in this section was so flat it presented a number of problems for the brigade and divisional staff compiling the defence plan. It was eventually covered by a trench line along the river bank, backed by eighteen machine-gun posts (36 Vickers guns) on the

***K.u.k.* 30.5 Howitzer.** FM

western slope of the Montello, supplemented by a brigade of field artillery installed in camouflaged positions in and around the deserted villages of Crocetta and Nogare. The guns covered much of the river bed from Pederobba to Falzè, and a large segment of the *Quartier del Piave*.

Support Weapons

The layout of the defences incorporated more machine-gun posts covering the river and possible enemy forming-up areas and approach routes on the *Quartier del Piave*. Additional fire-power was available from trench mortars in *dolini*, targeted on hillside gullies and dead ground along the river bank. Field guns and howitzers were also positioned in *dolini*, where the crews showed considerable ingenuity in digging emplacements, ammunition bays and shelters. Some machine-gun posts were also dug in *dolini* at the edge of the outer slopes of the hill, with firing ports at the end of tunnels; the guns and their crews safe from detection and virtually immune from artillery fire. The British troops, generally uninterrupted by enemy artillery fire or the unwelcome attention of *minenwerfer* and snipers, went to earth like moles.

Artillery in the Pederobba, Covolo and Montello sectors was linked in an integrated fire-plan which incorporated British, French and Italian field and heavy artillery, Italian mountain guns (on the Montello, under British command), mortars and machine guns. A similar fire-plan was prepared by the British and Italians for the area south of the Montello, covering the Nervesa-*Grave di Papadopoli* section. Enemy artillery in the copses and vineyards of the *Quartier del Piave* and in the hollows of the *Colli Susegana* opposite Nervesa were harassed by counter-battery fire, and quickly withdrew to safe ground. The *k.u.k.* responded with at least one 30.5 cm howitzer concealed behind a ridge out of range of most Allied guns; it caused some damage to billets in villages and farms, but the heavy shells proved almost useless in the soft soil and it was withdrawn for use in the mountains.

Intelligence

Intelligence collecting along the Piave received a powerful impetus when the British and French arrived, full of experience acquired on the Western Front. The defences on the river line were still flimsy and of little depth, and the CS remained convinced the enemy was going to continue the offensive. General Cavan and his staff, and their French colleagues, needed to know, quickly, the disposition, strength and order of battle of the enemy on the opposite bank to assess the probable threat. Information was acquired by a number of methods. Air reconnaissance (balloons or aircraft) was best, but German and Austrian fighters were active and it took time for the Allies to attain air parity, then air superiority, before their reconnaissance aircraft were able to search for dumps of bridging material and pontoons in the enemy rear areas. Initially, however, the Allies depended on ground-based observation: patrols into enemy held territory, SIGINT (signals intelligence) and long-range observation by telescope or camera. The Italian Military Intelligence Service, *Servizio Informazione d'Armata*, developed long-range photography for use on the Asiago Plateau area prior to the war to record the construction of Austrian frontier forts, at ranges of up to twenty kilometres. As soon as the British took over the front line they initiated, as a matter of routine, a corps-wide programme of reconnaissance patrols. These continued throughout the

Italian Army observers winter, only pausing when the Piave was in *piena*, flood, and filled the river bed from *bund* to *bund*. Immediately the enemy arrived on the Piave they established a line of outposts along the north bank. Most of these were visible from OPs on the Montello, but it was not clear how strong they were, or if they

Retractable k.u.k. searchlight illuminating an Italian church bell tower.
IWM 2/26

were manned at night, and the only way to find out was by crossing the river.

On the night of 3 December the first patrols checked the barbed wire barriers at the water's edge for flood damage and signs of tampering, while others passed through or round the wire and waded along its face to assess the depth and speed of the flow in the nearest channel. On 4 and 5 December patrols attempted to cross the channels to assess the possibility of siting outposts on shingle beds. These river crossing patrols were a new and unwelcome experience for the British troops, perhaps the worst many experienced during the war. The cold, fast, turbulent water was more dangerous than the enemy, who rarely took any interest in the proceedings. Every battalion quickly elected to carry the minimum amount of weapons, ammunition and equipment compatible with achieving a patrol's objectives. Most dispensed with helmets, adopting instead mufflers or balaclava helmets folded into warm and practical cap comforters. Some units favoured roping the patrol together, others tried holding knotted ropes or linking arms; others advocated thumb-sticks with wrist-loops, or long walking poles; many claimed the safest method was to slide the feet over the river bed rather than wading – anything to counter the force of the current. All units tried to ameliorate the effect of the cold water, including wearing felt or straw over-boots to insulate their feet. The CRE (Commander Royal Engineers) of XIV Corps, Major General FM Glubb, acquired some Berthon-type assault boats and skiffs to ferry patrols across the channels, the craft being man-handled across by working parties. When these vessels proved to be too heavy, unstable or unmanageable, improvised rafts were used, but were even less stable than the boats. Battalions experimented with ferrying patrol members across the channels on the backs of carrying parties of a new and novel kind, but found that to be dangerous for everyone involved. The only sure method of crossing the Piave was wading, and again many attempts were made to counter the cold. These included rubbing the bodies and limbs with whale oil or thick grease, which proved to be not only nearly useless against the cold but very unpleasant, and almost impossible to remove in the primitive living conditions of the trenches. Thigh-high gum boots pulled over very thick socks seems to have been the best method of reducing the effect of the cold. But, nothing really solved the problem. Patrolling meant wading bitterly cold water, getting wet, and freezing almost to death. Few men were required to cross the Piave twice, but many privates and NCOs volunteered to do so; junior officers were expected to carry out a number of patrols as a matter of course. Crossing the river was not helped by the Austrian habit of shining searchlights across the waters at random intervals, accompanied by bursts of machine-gun fire. From early December blizzards made life even more unpleasant.

A map prepared on 1 January 1918 by the Intelligence Section, GHQ BEF (I) of patrol activity during December marks the date and route of twenty-five; of them eight were deemed successful, in that they reached the enemy bank. The abbreviated reports include references to the depth and speed of the water. The channels, or streams, were reported to be anything from three to six feet deep, and the current as very strong; *current about 14 miles per hour; water waist deep; branch of main stream crossed – width 25 yds depth 2 1/2 feet; strong current, rope used, main stream 30 to 40 yds wide; strong current crossed by 1 officer 1 NCO remainder of patrol swept off their feet although using ropes.*

Montebelluna church used as a motor-fuel store, 1918

Pederiva ridge; artillery hides, north-east face.

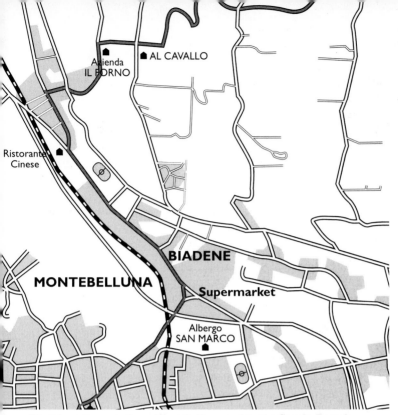

The Montello route from Montebelluno and to the Strada Dorsale.

TOUR ROUTE C:
The Montello
December 1917 - March 1918
Start: Caerano roundabout
Maps: LAC **Treviso**, BericaEditrice *Il Montello*

Itinerary: At the roundabout take the **SS248** for **Montebelluna**. After 4 kms watch out on the right for a splendid brick-built church, half-complete in Norman Gladden's time, and used as a store for motor fuel in 1918, whilst the forecourt housed supply and admin elements of HQ XIV Corps.

Continue further into the town, watching for signs pointing left for **Biadene**, and head through some small streets and up a shallow slope in a cutting. This is carved through the crescent-shaped ridge mentioned above, the Pederiva. In 1917 the northern face of the ridge was burrowed with artillery hides, the top entrenched and the wooded slopes laced with barbed wire.

Montello: The Soldiers' Fountain, Strada Dorsale. FM

There is a small village, Mercato Vecchio, on the ridge west of the cutting. Each year, near the end of August, Montebelluna organizes the *Palio di Vecchio Mercato*, a race around the town between teams from different neighbourhoods, each drawing a market cart loaded with merchandise once typical of the locality. The route includes a lung-bursting haul up to the top of ridge, and an exciting and dangerous run back down. The *palio* is a great spectacle, but many streets in Montebelluna are closed throughout the weekend, and for several evenings beforehand for practice runs, so keep an eye open for *deviazione* signs.

Biadene

Drive over the brow of the hill and under a railway bridge to a junction. Go straight ahead, and into a small one-way system; on the right hand side is a good supermarket, handy for picnic supplies. (When the Piave ran this way it was navigable almost as far this point, and to the right was a Roman port, at Caonada.)

Bear left at the junction or when leaving the supermarket, and head through Biadene. After about 300 metres look out on the right for a large church and quadrangle which in 1918 housed a YMCA hut, much appreciated by the soldiers.

Drive on, bear right at the road fork and start looking right immediately for a street sign marked *Presa 21: Via Gandolfo*. Turn right into the *presa*. After about 100 metres it crosses a water channel, the *Canale del Bosco*, deeper (three metres in places) and colder than it appears on a summer morning. It was originally dug to drain the ground around Crocetta, then enlarged by tapping water from the Piave above Covolo to float timber from the Montello down to Nervesa for rafting to Venice.

Montello: view of the Grappa *massif*, the *Colli Àsolani* and the Monfenera Ridge. FM

After crossing the channel take *Presa 21* up onto the Montello; turn right at the first cross roads onto the ***Strada Dorsale***. In 1918 the area to the right was a British training area, 'A'; Training Area B was on the slope behind Biadene, near the foot of *Presa 17*. The training areas were used day and night by battalions in the left brigade reserve position for practising counter-attack procedures, simple fire and maneouvre tactics and dry weapon training.

Continue up the *Strada Dorsale* past ***Presa 19 Via Brigata Campania*** and ***Presa 18 Via V. Fiorone.*** After 200 metres the road crosses a stretch of meadow; there is a small picnic area on the left at the bend in the road which provides a splendid view to the Grappa *massif*, the M. Tomba – Monfenera ridge, and the *Colli Àsolani*. On the bend there is a spring-fed horse trough, marked on maps as the ***Fonte Caldiera Peduoia***, but referred to by the locals as *The Soldiers' Fountain*. The water is cold and very refreshing on a hot day, and apparently rarely freezes in winter; in 1917/18 it was frequently used by British draught horses and by soldiers bivouacked in nearby *dolini*. Continue up the *Strada Dorsale* for about 50 metres from the drinking trough into a left-hand bend; look-out for traffic emerging, left or right,

Montello: View from the farmhouse used in 1918 by British troops as an OP. FM

from *Presa 17: Via Lollini*. Turn left into the *Presa*, which is surfaced for about a kilometre and then becomes a dirt-track. It serves a number of small-holdings and houses, many established in the 1870s. In 1866 the Austrians lost control of the Veneto, and the Italian government or, more accurately, the Veneto regional authority, made vigorous attempts to improve the economy of the Treviso region, the *Marca Trevigiana*, after years of Austrian neglect. These efforts included redistribution of land on the Montello, some of which remains in the hands of families who were recipients of the first land grants.

Near the bottom of the *presa* is one such small holding, still farmed but more as family vegetable patch than as a full-time occupation. In 1918 the farmhouse was used by British observers as it provided excellent views across the front of the left forward brigade sector as far as Vidor, and across the *Quartier del Piave*. In June 2000 the owner of the small holding, a retired construction worker, showed the author and his wife around the small holding and the buildings. He was a mine of information about the area, and its role in the Great War. At one time he had a large collection of bombs, shells, shrapnel, grenades, bullets, barbed wire, steel helmets, water bottles and mess tins, but they became so corroded and fractured that he disposed of them, as did many of his nieghbours who had also uncovered a steel harvest over the years. He also explained that the bed of the Piave is now considerably narrower than in 1918 due to extraction of shingle for building material in the post-war housing booms of the early 1920s and late 40s, and the recent growth of light industry in the Veneto. Climatic changes have reduced snowfalls in the Dolomites so the sudden floods and torrents which impressed the British are mainly a thing of the past.

The small holder also provided a tour of his garden, full of vegetable plots and also a large wire cage of *bobolo*, the local name for very large edible snails; an offer of lunch was gracefully declined.

The last stretch of *Presa 17* is very steep and there is a sharp corner where it reaches a cross-roads where the *Presa* cuts road circumnavigating the Montello; this road is much used by mountain bikers and motorcyclists, fast but harmless, and walkers and horse riders, slow and chatty.

At the foot of *Presa 17* the village of **Ciano di Piave** is just visible on the left and, nearer to hand, lies the community cemetery, near the foot of **Presa 18 Via V. Fiorone**. The cemetery was used by at least one British unit during the winter of 1917/18 to bury men killed in the front line by enemy gunfire, or who died of disease, natural causes, or as the result of an accident. During the night of 9/10 January 1918 one such accident was seen by Norman Gladden:

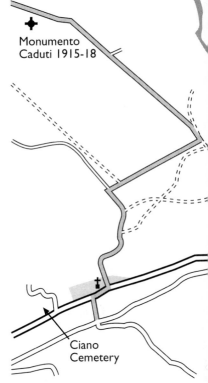

In the early hours of the morning a fire suddenly burst forth from a neighbouring post...I went along to investigate. Flames were issuing from a dug-out, whose sides, revetted with brushwood, were burning like tinder.. Only later did we learn the details of the tragedy. One of the dug-out's occupants had accidentally kicked over a brazier while still sleeping, and the fire got a hold so rapidly that one of his colleagues had been caught like a rat in a trap and burned to death.

The victim was Private Thomas Walker, of Newcastle-upon-Tyne. He was eventually laid to rest in Giavera CWGC Cemetery; where the register records that he *died of accidental injuries* on 10 January 1918. The War Diary of 11/Northumberland Fusiliers recorded that Pte Walker of 'C' Coy burned himself to death in his dugout in the front line. Court of Enquiry held – quiet day.

The Montello. Access to Presa 17 and the Grave Di Ciano.

At the main road, nowadays the **Strada Panoramica** but once the 'Cliff Road' of War Diaries, turn right, watch for a shrine on the left, and then a signpost for *Monumento Caduti 1915-1918*, pointing down a lane, also on the left.

Grave di Ciano

Turn right into the lane. This crosses an irrigation channel, and descends to what in 1918 was the river bed. The third lane on the right leads to an impressive memorial, the *Monumento Caduti 1915-1918* which commemorates the dead of various engagements along the Piave, from the arrival of the Austrians and Germans to the Battle of Vittorio Veneto. It is a quiet, solitary and poignant spot; very quiet on an autumn morning, and well worth a visit for its own sake. But from the point of view of the British forces on the Montello, the monument lies on what was once the eastern shore of the *Grave di Ciano*, an area crossed by British patrols heading for the *k.u.k.* outposts on the far bank. Norman Gladden described one such patrol across this stretch in graphic terms. He gives the date as 8 January 1918, and that it was led by his platoon commander, a newly-commissioned novice, but the War Diary of 11/Northumberland Fusiliers has no record of a patrol on that day. However, on 6 January a patrol from C Company (Gladden's) tried to cross the Piave. It included, unusually, two officers: an experienced subaltern, Lieutenant J Moffat MC, and a Second Lieutenant Petrie, possibly Gladden's platoon commander 'under instruction'. Gladden notes that the patrol consisted of fifteen men, and included a two man Lewis gun team consisting of Privates Westgarth, the No. 1 (gunner), and Gladden. (The term 'Fusilier' was not adopted until the 1920s.) The patrol did not wear steel helmets or carry gas masks; everyone carried a rifle and a single cloth bandolier of ammunition, except Westgarth with the Lewis gun and Gladden with the ammunition drums. Everyone wore only underwear, socks, boots and canvas overalls, coloured white for disguise against the snow and the shingle beds. To continue in Norman Gladden's words:

> Thus garbed we crossed the trench zone...white ghosts rather than men, as voices from our advance posts hailed us and without envy wished us the best of luck. It was not a dark night: the bright snow reflected back an unearthly sort of light across the shingle. The cold was intense and we were hardly dressed to cope with it.

And,

> We waded the first stream, a gliding torrent of icy water not more than a foot deep. Hitherto the scrunchy snow had struck a deep chilliness through my boots; now the icy bath penetrated to the skin and took away all feeling from my legs...We now reached the most formidable obstacle. A much bigger stream, some thirty yards or so across, now obstructed our progress, and we began with little thought to wade across. It was shallow at first, like the previous streams, but deepened towards the middle. The water was now swirling nearly to our waists. Now surely it would get shallower, but as we approached the opposite bank the waters continued to rise and the current to rush upon us with terrific spate. Taken completely by surprise, I found myself struggling up to my neck. The man just ahead of me had been swept from his feet and only just managed to strike the shore where it jutted out into the torrent. I had a similar experience. For a few moments I completely lost my balance and felt myself swirling along helplessly like a cork. It was touch and go, for I was no great swimmer. I saw the bank coming up towards me and then, when

right in the grip of the eddy, a hand shot out and I found myself scrambling up the shingle to safety...The noise of the main stream was now becoming audible above all other sound. The officer, accompanied by an NCO and a runner, went forward to reconnoitre...(it) was so swollen by the recent rains and running like a mill-race, that it constituted an impassable barrier between us and the enemy. (The War Diary records that the fighting patrol under Lieutenant Moffat found the water in the last stream too deep to cross.)

The patrol retraced their steps, and crossed the wide channel by linking arms and shuffling across. Once in their own lines the patrol were taken to Battalion Forward (Battle) HQ, located in a house behind the rearmost support trench. A room had been laid out as a sort of Turkish bath, with half-barrels full of hot water; Italian trench stores put to good use. The frozen soldiers were helped out of their sodden overalls and lifted into the barrels. After they had thawed out the men received dry underclothing, a warm blanket and a good tot of rum, and immediately entered into oblivion. All, that is, but the platoon commander and his 'apprentice', who had to be debriefed and then help the Battalion Intelligence Officer up-date large-scale charts of the river bed.

Identification

The mission of most patrols was to locate enemy defence posts and wire along the north bank of the river, and to establish which were occupied and in what manner, (OPs, listening or machine-gun nests, bases for 'sweep' patrols). Patrols tried to capture at least one prisoner, or at least acquire cap badges, shoulder straps with regimental numbers or some other form of unit identification. *K.u.k.* soldiers were not issued with name tags. They carried a metal clip, a holder for their *Legitmationskarte*. This was an invaluable document for intelligence officers, as it not only not only identified the soldier, but his present unit and record of service; very useful for interrogators when preparing an 'interview'. These cards were the soldiers only means of identification so had to be returned once 'name, rank and number' had been recorded in prisoner of war registers.

Return to the *Strada Panoramica* and turn left.

Front Line Defences

These ran along the line of the *Strada Panoramica* and, wherever the road goes, so once did British soldiers. There is a water channel beside

Cliff Road: Cippo della Arditi. Dale Hjort

the road, the *Canale della Vittoria*, used for irrigation and to power a hydro-electric plant at Nervesa. It was built after the Great War by Austrian prisoners of war and its construction filled in many of the support and communication trenches, work completed when Cliff Road was straightened, widened, surfaced and renamed.

This section of the front line also had its share of patrol actions. In the PRO file number WO95/4238, the 10/Duke of Wellington's War Diary has as an appendix to the entry for 1 March 1918 the following:

Report of patrol carried out by the 10th Bn., D.O.W.'s. Regt., on the night of 28th Feb./1st March 1918 Reference Map: Moriago 1:20,000. Strength of patrol: 3 Officers, 20 men divided as follows into three parties: a) 1 Ofr (2/Lt. AJ Acarnley), 12 OR. b) 1 Ofr (2/Lt. MAS Wood), 4 OR. c) 1 Ofr (2/Lt. A Allen),4 O.R.

a) *To proceed Due North (Magnetic) to reconnoitre the enemy wire & if possible M.PILONETTO.*

b) *To proceed True North with the same object as No.1 patrol but not to go beyond the wire..*

c) *To proceed with No.2 party as far as the wire and then to reconnoitre for 500 yards Due East.*

Action by the patrol: All three parties were across the river by 7.25pm and ready to start.

(1) Action of the First Party: The party proceeded rather to the West of Magnetic North and after searching the scrub were confronted by a stretch of shingle between them and the river bank. The Officer here decided to go forward with three men to see whether it was possible for the remainder of the patrol to follow. While engaged in crawling across the shingle an enemy post of 4 men was observed. The 4 men then divided into 2 pairs and crawled further forward. Hereupon they were observed and a man came slightly out from the shadow of the bank. Not satisfied with what he saw he went back and came forward with a second man. They came to within four or five yards of the Officer who fired his revolver point blank at the first man. This man, although apparently hit in the stomach, immediately closed

with the Officer while the remaining man of the post ran back to give the alarm. Apparently they had not far to go as machine gun fire and rifle fire were opened in very quick time. The wounded man was apparently quite off his head and struggled with great vigour with the Officer and a Sergeant who were together. Eventually he got away but not before his cap had been secured. The party then collected and after making a short reply to the fire aimed at them returned without casualties. It is believed that the skirmish took place at about H.28.28.

The document continues to account for the two other patrol, which by comparison were uneventful. The patrol was back in their own lines by 10.30 pm. The Report is signed by Major JC Bull, O.C. 'B' Coy.

The *London Gazette* later reported the following awards:

10th Duke of Wellington's (West Riding Regt.), 69 Inf.Bde., 23 Division.

Citation for the honour granted for patrolling across the River Piave on the Montello front, on the night 28th February/1st March 1918:

Military Cross: Second Lieutenant AJ Acarnley: 'For conspicuous gallantry and devotion to duty. When he was in command of a patrol reconnoitring the farther side of the river his position was discovered, but owing to his good leadership and initiative, he succeeded in withdrawing his patrol without loss. His patrol work at all times has been most conspicuous and during numerous crossings of the river he has displayed great courage and skill.'

The Machin map *(see page 64).*

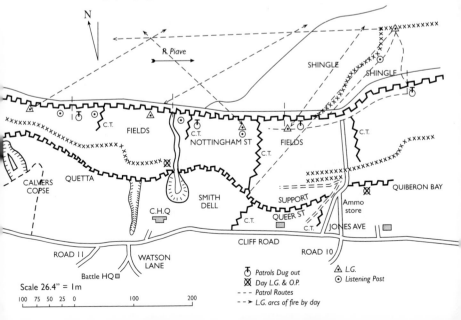

Cippo Della Arditi

Drive to the **Trattoria Cippo degli Arditi**, handy for coffee and parking. It also has, or had as of autumn 2000, a small display of material relating to the nearby cippo, a memorial in the shape of a broken Roman column. The memorial lies about seventy metres west of *Presa 12 Via S. Martino*. The Cippo commemorates the exploits of a detachment of *Arditi*, commandos, at the start of the Battle of Vittorio Veneto. *Arditi* were mainly armed with daggers and grenades, and carried a carbine to hold off enemy counter-attacks until supporting infantry arrived to take over trenches. The team crossed the Piave ahead of the main force to clear enemy trenches near a bridging site, but were decimated when their infantry supports were delayed by damaged bridges.

Crocetta Sub-Sector - *The Machin Map*

Beyond the trattoria and the start of *Presa 11 Via Sernaglia*, can be found the ground illustrated on a sketch map made by Second Lieutenant James Machin, 18/KRRC, during December 1917. A few metres along from *Presa 11* is a minor road which equates to 'Watson Lane' and the first house on the left was probably the site of the Battalion Command Post. Opposite Watson Lane a cart track runs down a gully leading to the river. A metal bridge carries the Canale della Vittorio over the track, one of the few routes between *Prese 15* and *8* where farmers or walkers can reach the river. The track degenerates into a footpath which will take the determined walker to the *bund*, exactly where James Machin placed Nottingham Street. A local farmer states that signs of concrete parapets, and indications of communications trenches, can be seen after a heavy snow fall or a summer brush fire. Standing on the *bund* where a sentry or patrol commander would have stood on a winter dawn, the tourist can gain an impression of the view across the riverbed to the *Quartier del Piave*. The change in the topography of the riverbed can also be appreciated as the main channel is now nearly 600 metres. away, not twenty as in 1918.

Return to the *Strada Panoramic*. The house on the left at the top of the gully was almost certainly the site of Company Headquarters (CHQ on the Machin map). In 2000 the owners remembered hearing about *inglesi* and the *grande guerra mondiale*, but could provide no information; none of the family spoke English, and while courteous appeared to relish their privacy.

The construction of the *Canale* and the *Strada Panoramica* seems to have obliterated the support trench, Quetta/Queer Street/Quiberon

Bay on the map. There are no signs of trenches in the area of the Company HQ house, apart from some odd cavities and the barbed wire. But thanks to the map drawn by Second Lieutenant James Machin, anyone wanting to visit a spot where their predecessors spent long cold days, and longer nights, beside the Piave in the last winter of the Great War can do so by way of the gully opposite Watson Lane; but not necessarily in January!

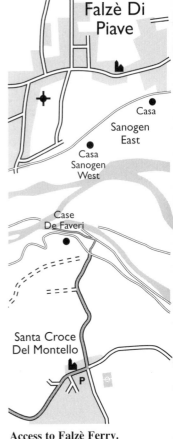

Access to Falzè Ferry.

Falzè Ford and Ferry

Continue along the **Strada Panoramica**, which gradually climbs to the top of the Montello and to the village of **Santa Croce del Montello**. Drive as far as the crossroads in the centre of the village and park in the car park opposite the church. The war memorial by the car park is for the *Raggazi di' 99*, conscripts born in 1899 and killed along the Piave. It is worth parking and walking down to the site of the ferry as the road eventually becomes very narrow. Go down the road opposite the large war memorial to a cluster of buildings, the *Case de Faveri*. By the time the British ventured down here to set up an OP, they were little more than rubble. But here was a space underneath, little more than a vestige of one of the cellars, and it was turned into an OP; it gave good views of the *k.u.k.* garrison in **Falzè de Piave**, but was difficult to reach even at night as the enemy swept the face of the Montello with searchlights, backed up with artillery and machine-guns.

Follow the path to the right of the houses through the woods cloaking the steep slope above the river and down to the river. There is, in theory, a ford here, crossing to what is now a small *grave*. On an old map there is a ferry symbol on this location, and this was where British patrols crossed the river to raid enemy posts around Falzè. The aim of the patrols was to make sure the enemy were not attempting to stockpile bridging equipment, or preparing a raid or offensive.

Extract from the WD of 12/Gloucesters:

Report of Fighting Patrol carried out on night of 23/24 February 1918 by 'C' Company 12th Gloucestershire Regiment.

1. The Fighting Patrol was the third of a series of attacks upon the enemy's advanced posts, all being carried out on consecutive nights in very much the same locality owing to there being one ford across the River Piave.

2. The general idea on which these fighting patrols was based was that: a) It was considered advisable to force the enemy to withdraw his advanced posts; b) To take prisoners from, or inflict as many casualties as possible on, the enemy.

3. The special idea was that an enemy Machine Gun was suspected at a point about 150 to 200 yards West of CASA SANOGEN WEST, (information from prisoners captured on night of 22/23rd February 1918) and patrol was to capture it.

4. A machine gun barrage was arranged; 3 machine guns doing [sic] indirect fire on enemy's line on NORTHERN side of road between j.230/125 and j.280/110 and one machine gun covering each flank so as to make a rough box-barrage.

5. Occasional bursts of Lewis Gun fire were to be opened to prevent enemy hearing movements of patrol and to keep their heads down.

6. Discretion was left to OC Patrol to capture any suitable post he might encounter.

7. Patrol consisted of 2nd Lt. WJ Hale, 12 Other Ranks (of these three men were left to hold the Ford) and 1 Signaller whose function was to flash a light when barrage was required.

8. Patrol left our lines at 6.30 pm., crossed River PIAVE by the Ford; and returned: 1st party of 8 other ranks carrying 1 Other Rank wounded about 8.10pm. 2nd party 3 Other Ranks and 2nd Lt HALE at 8.15 pm.

9. Casualties: Ours. 1 Other Rank missing believed killed. 1 Other Rank wounded. Enemy's. At least 5 believed killed by patrol, also many casualties should have been caused by machine gun fire, by Lewis gun fire, and about 5 rounds rapid from about 40 men when patrol came in.

10. After crossing River, patrol (now 1 Officer and 10 Other Ranks strong, leaving 3 Other Ranks at Ford as covering party) made for a point about 200 yards West of C. SANOGEN W. to search for enemy machine gun. On their way they searched every post they came to; these, as well as suspected machine gun post, were empty. Patrol then proceeded along the bank to near C. SANOGEN E. finding no trace of the enemy.

They then again proceeded to C. SANOGEN W. and seeing 4

of the enemy approaching, lay down in two holes and awaited their arrival. The party of four apparently saw them and bolted, crying 'PRESTO ITALIANI' or something similar. Patrol then moved to a point about 200 yards EAST of C. SANOGEN W., searching posts again and still finding them unoccupied. Patrol next moved again towards C. SANOGEN W. Suddenly, a very strong party of the enemy (estimated at about 100 strong) made their appearance from track near C. SANOGEN W. They were in a very close bunched up formation and ran towards the patrol, the front men firing as they ran (at the word of command of an Officer).

Patrol immediately opened rapid fire – enemy were about 20 yards away – and at the first burst 5 Hungarians fell groaning. Fighting continued for about 5 or 10 minutes with bullet and bayonet.

Patrol Commander seeing he was outnumbered gave the order to withdraw. He and 3 Other Ranks remained as covering party and retreated along bank towards C. SANOGEN E. so as to bring enfilade fire to bear on any enemy pursuing remainder of patrol.

5 Other Ranks withdrew (carrying one of the patrol who had been wounded) firing on the enemy as they went.

The covering party now withdrew in pairs. 2nd Lt HALE was left with No.27905 Pte. M Tucker covering withdrawal of covering party. Pte. Tucker suddenly exclaimed 'I am done for' and fell forward on his face. 2nd Lt. HALE rushed forward to his assistance but he was immediately surrounded by a number of the enemy. His rifle jammed but he fought his way clear with his fists. (During this time enemy appeared to have been considerably re-inforced.) Our Machine gun barrage now increased to 'Rapid Fire'; this apparently frightened the enemy and checked their pursuit. As soon as the patrol reached the Ford, fire was opened with Lewis Guns on the enemy's River bank. When patrol reached our side of the Ford, 5 rounds 'Rapid Fire' was also opened by about 40 men on the chance of hitting any of the enemy.

11. In conclusion I would submit that in view of the brilliant moonlight, the rattling of the pebbles, making a noiseless movement almost impossible, and the fact that the enemy, having already lost posts on two successive evenings were very much on the alert, the patrol did good work under very difficult

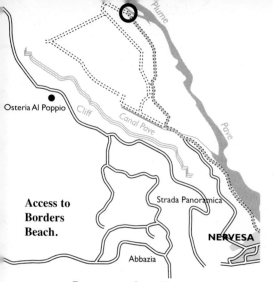

circumstances and I consider that having regard to the comparatively heavy casualties inflicted on the enemy, such patrols have an undoubted value and should be continued. A raid would, however, be even better.

Signed (HA COLT, MC)
Lt Col Commanding,
12/Gloucesters

Cliff Defences

Return to the village, and continue along the *Strada Panoramica* towards Nervesa. Parking along this stretch of road is not easy, apart from the car park of the ***Osteria Ai Pioppi***, about 1km from San Croce. In late January 1918, 20 Brigade (7th Division) manned this section of the front line, sometimes referred to as 'the Gorge'as it overlooks a defile cut by the Piave. In the immediate vicinity of the *Osteria* was 2/Border, nominally the support battalion but in the front line. 2/Gordon were in the Nervesa section to the Borders' right, and 8/Devons on the left, around San Croce, the 9/Devons in reserve on the south side of the Montello, in Bavaria, a small village near the southern end of ***Presa 2 Via Alessi.***

A brief but eloquent description of the Gorge section of the front line appears in *The Border Regiment in the Great War:*

> ...the front companies each had two platoons below the cliff on the shore and islands, with their Company Headquarters at heads of Roads 2 and 3 respectively. Battalion Headquarters in a cottage on the extreme right of Road 2 with dug-outs in a neighbouring hollow. The troops below the cliff occupy fifteen posts by the water's edge and spend the time wiring and improving their positions. The ground occupied is covered with scrub and small trees which hide the day positions, shelters and dug-outs, 50 to 500 yards behind the posts. The river is divided into three to eight streams of varying width and depth, but all are very swift. Except for scrub near the foreshore, the river bed is of shingle, gleaming white by day, with ribbons of blue water threading through it. Posts can only be visited at night, with the exception of two Observation Posts on the cliff. 'D' Company's

68

Headquarters are in a big cave near the base of the cliff approached by a goat-track. The other ways to the shore are the mule-track and quarry steps.

Note: the area below the cliff can be reached from Nervesa, but as of 1999 it was a vast expanse of scrub and rough pasture, with some scattered plantations and woods. The river bank where the British outposts were located is accessible, with difficulty due to undergrowth, on a bearing of 225 degrees from the 'beach' to the scarcely visible roof of the *Osteria;* and that was in winter, when there was little vegetation.

Tour D
Nervesa, Giavera Cemetery & Memorial to the Missing, The Arcade Sector

Introduction

Drive into ***Nervesa Della Battaglia.*** There are several good parking places in the middle of the town. Walk to the traffic lights in the middle of the town; the river Piave is beyond a bridge over the tail-race from a hydro-electric plant north of the town, water from the *Canale della Vittorio.* At the *bund* there is small memorial to an Italian gun team which during the *Battaglia del Solstizio* (15-23 June 1918) fought to the last round and the last man; the battered field gun forms part of the memorial. The plaque records:

> *IN QUESTI LUOGHI IL 16G 1918 ARTIGLIERI DELLA IVa*
> *BATTERIA DEL 14a REGIMENTO DA CAMPPAGNALA*
> *ESAURITE LE MUNIZIONI, COLPITO DAL FUOCO*
> *NEMICO IL CANNONE, SU QUESTO CADEVANO ESTREMO*
> *BALUARDO DI VITTORIOSA DIFESA*

Roughly:

> *In this place on the 16th June 1918 artillery of the 4th Battery,*
> *14th Field Regiment, out of ammunition and with the gun*

69

Nervesa della Battaglia; Italian artillery memorial. FM

knocked out by enemy fire, died while acting as final bulwark in a victorious defence.

Austrian Pontoon

Walk along the path at the edge of the *bund* for a couple of hundred metres to a small display of military relics. These contain what is, according to locals, the only surviving example of a *k.u.k.* pontoon. Apparently a few years ago the Austrian government asked if it could

Nervesa della Battaglia; the last *k.u.k.* pontoon. FM

be returned; the request was politely declined. The pontoon was apparently recovered from the bed of the river after the final withdrawal of *k.u.k.* units from the Montello in June 1918. It is a bow section, and could either be bolted back to back with another to make to make a small pontoon or an assault boat. One or more centre sections could be inserted for making large bridging pontoons for vehicle and railway bridges.

Return to the car, and drive back towards Nervesa, and follow the signs for Montebelluna along the **SS248**.

Giavera

Drive into Giavera and, approaching a shallow bend to the right about four kilometres from Nervesa, look on the side of the road for a CWGC sign pointing right; or, the on the right side for a signpost for the *Antico Trattoria Agnoletti*, along the *Via Vittorio*, on the right. Turn into Via Vittorio and at the end turn left, then right at the CWGC sign, and up the hill towards the church. The entrance to the CWGC cemetery is almost opposite the entrance to the car park. There is a short walk along a path lined with young trees; beautiful in summer or autumn. The cemetery is perhaps the most serene of all the CWGC sites in Northern Italy, and is a very dignified and beautiful place, summer or winter. The Great Cross faces the entrance; the MEMORIAL TO THE MISSING ON THE ITALIAN FRONT is on a terrace to the left, a small shelter housing a wall cabinet for the

Giavera CWGC Cemetery. FM

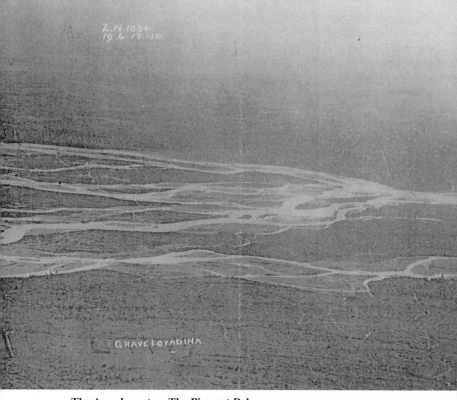

GRAVE LOYADINA.

The Arcade sector: The Piave at Palazzon. Worcestershire Regt

Cemetery Register and the Visitors Book, which holds few British but many Italian names, as with all of the CWGC cemeteries in the Veneto.

The Memorial to the Missing was sited so as to command a view of the Asiago Plateau, the Montello and the Piave. The Asiago Plateau can only be glimpsed nowadays in winter, from the left hand top corner below the shelter, when the trees in the little valley beyond the north wall are bare of leaf. But it can be glimpsed – just.

Among those buried here are Private Walker, the Northumberland Fusilier who died in the burning dug-out near Ciano, and 285129 Private Frederick George Stevenson, 2/Gordons, 20 Brigade, 7th Division. Private Stevenson was killed on 5 February 1918, in Nervesa. The battalion was in reserve. It was billeted in Bavaria, a few kilometres east of Giavera and at the southern end of *Presa* 2, which provided direct access to the brigade's front line positions around the *Osteria Ai Pioppi*. Fred Stevenson was in A Company, and on 5 February was one of a working party sent to Nervesa to assist one of the divisional RE Field Companies strengthen defences in and around the town. Fred was busy in D Work, a strongpoint under construction in the ruins of the town near the river when *k.u.k.* artillery in the hills opposite the town, the *Colli Susegana*, took advantage of the good weather to fire a short barrage into the town. To quote the Battalion WD; *'A shell pitched amongst working party of 'A' Coy working on D work, killing 3 and wounding 3, one of whom has died of wounds.'* Apart from Fred Stevenson, the Gordons lost Privates JJ Donlan, J McLean, and Serjeant William Forbes Thomson. William Thomson was a member of 'A' Company and 28 years old when killed. He was the husband of Alice Evelyn Thomson, of Mains of Whitehall, New Deer, Aberdeenshire; and the son of Alexander and Isabella Thomson, of Fetterangus, Aberdeenshire. He is buried in Plot 2, Row D, Grave 4; Privates Donlan and McLean are in Graves 5 and 6. Fred Stevenson is buried in the same plot, but in Row C, Grave 4, so it is probable he was the soldier who died of wounds sustained in the enemy barrage. None of the Privates have any personal information in the Register or on the headstone. By one of these strange coincidences familiar to anyone researching the Great War, the grand-daughter of Fred Stevenson was put in contact with the author during the week this section was being revised, hence the information about his life and times, and the death of the four Gordon Highlanders.

The Arcade Sector

In early December 1917 the British were asked to deploy XI Corps into the line on the right of XIV Corps, to relieve VIII (It) Corps in the Arcade sector, named after the nearest town. The 5th Division entered the line and assumed operational control on 27 January. 95 Brigade took over the sector from 48th Italian Division, 1/East Surreys relieved the 216th Italian Infantry Regiment in the Palazzon sub-sector, north-east of Spresiano; with 12/Gloucesters to their right, 1/DCLI in support at Spresiano and 1/Devon Regt in reserve at Visnadello.

The Corps remained in the sector until March 1918 when

Arcade sector: Piave front line trench, British soldiers and an Italian sentry, pose for a publicity shot.

it returned to France, albeit having exchanged the 48th Division for the 41st, which went to France with the 5th Division. The sector extended from Nervesa to Palazzon, opposite the upper end of a large island, the *Grave di Papadopoli*, which later that year became well-known to British troops in the opening rounds of the Battle of Vittorio Veneto.

Trenches

The trench routine in this sector was quieter than on the Montello, as the river was rather too wide (up to 2,000 metres in the spring floods) to wade. The trenches inherited from the Italians required constant work, as they were dug into the soft earth of the landward face of the *bund*, or in vineyards behind it. The forward trenches were described in *The 5th Division in the Great War* as consisting of T heads, with machine-gun posts run forward into the retaining walls of the rivers.

THE REAR AREAS
or
SCHOOLS AND MULES

Introduction

As soon as the Allies arrived in Italy, staff officers began working with the Military Missions and the CS to develop training schools. Topics discussed included the provision of host-nation support: requisitioned land; supply of building materials and labour; provisions and fodder; and access to water supplies, especially the question of riparian rights in farming areas where irrigation was a necessity. Also discussed were terms of employment for locally recruited direct labour, compensation for damage, loss of crops or animals and injury to civilians. These terms were needed immediately as local training was quickly started, or continued from where it had been interrupted by the journey to Italy. For example, given the clear air in Italy and the certainty that operations would be conducted in the mountains, the 48th Divisional Signal Company ran Visual Signalling (Morse code by electric hand lamp or heliograph and semaphore signalling with hand-held flags) courses.

It was agreed among the three Allied nations that they would open their courses to each other's personnel, but for a number of reasons that

Allied Training Areas and Schools 1918.

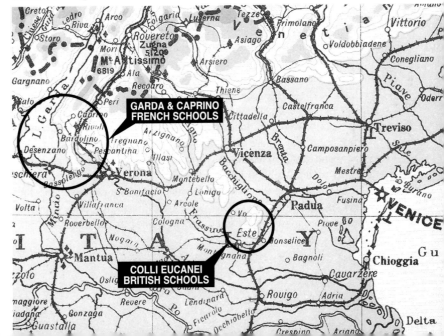

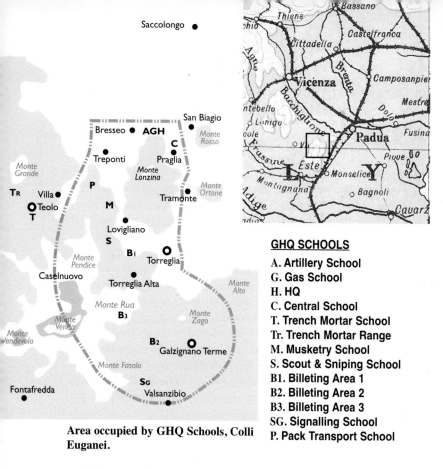

Area occupied by GHQ Schools, Colli Euganei.

GHQ SCHOOLS

A. Artillery School
G. Gas School
H. HQ
C. Central School
T. Trench Mortar School
Tr. Trench Mortar Range
M. Musketry School
S. Scout & Sniping School
B1. Billeting Area 1
B2. Billeting Area 2
B3. Billeting Area 3
SG. Signalling School
P. Pack Transport School

rarely happened. For example, an Italian Army school for artillery subalterns based in the requisitioned Palazzo Morandi in Malo, north of Vicenza, accepted as students two French junior artillery officers who spoke some Italian. But, the language problem, and differences in weapons, gunnery techniques and even some key aspects of the surveying techniques required in wooded mountains (different from the hills of the Vosges and Jura, and in some ways from the French Alps) saw the exchange terminated early – without recrimination. Better results were obtained by staff visits between units and joint planning sessions, where the Italians learned a lot about co-ordinating infantry and artillery plans, and British and French gunners acquired the skills to deal with mountain warfare.

In late May 1918 the Italians stopped sending any students to the British and French schools. This was partly a response to the growing evidence from a number of intelligence sources that a major Austrian offensive was imminent, and the CS wanted to ensure that all front line and reserve divisions were fully manned. The Italians also felt, with some justification, that as officers and NCOs attending French or British schools were trained in techniques different from those used in their parent units and formations, they emerged with lessened faith in their own training and methods and with an incomplete knowledge of those of their allies. And, in any case, British and French methods would rarely be used by Italian arms or services. Also the CS intended starting a central training school; date and location unspecified.

By 31 December 1917 both expeditionary forces had selected sites, partly based on access to railways so that in an emergency students, staff and weapons could be moved into the battle area. The two forces had slightly different requirements, mainly due to the arrival of the two French divisions of mountain infantry, the *Chasseurs Alpin*, and their organic artillery, engineering and supply units.

French Schools
The Tenth Army established two schools near Lake Garda, with a direct rail connection to Verona. The main site was near the lake-side resort of Garda which was, and is, well-endowed with hotels. Some were in use by personnel from Italian 'coastal' artillery posts. The upper end of the lake remained in Austrian hands, and both sides patrolled a watery front line with miniature navies of armed motor boats, the occasional skirmish – bursts of machine-gun fire – keeping the management happy.

A second site, mainly used by the *Chassuers Alpin* units, was found at Caprino, a small market town-cum-resort at the foot of the M. Baldo *massif*. Here the French established a mountain training area where the Chassuers could practise the tactics peculiar to fighting and living on a sloping battlefield. Training included moving guns and limbers over rocks, crevices, slopes and cliffs. There was also an artillery range, where guns of different calibres, firing a mix of ammunition types, were co-ordinated in simulated set-piece attacks, counter-battery missions, and interdicting enemy attacks. The French instructors and staff artillery officers also examined the Italian methods of fire-control, gun positions and ammunition natures when fighting in mountain forests and, like their British colleagues, profited from studying and adopting or adapting their techniques.

The French schools were run by staff drawn from the Instruction Centres (CID: *Centre d'Instruction Divisionale*) of each division in Tenth Army. The CID of an infantry division was commanded by a

77

Lieutenant Colonel, and manned by an HQ consisting of a small group of training and administrative officers, warrant officers and NCOs, a squadron of cavalry for demonstration and administrative duties, and several squadrons of engineer/pioneer troops to prepare ranges, trenches, barbed wire defences and dug-outs. Artillery and machine-gun teams were provided in turn by the divisions using the schools. The CID for a *Chasseur Alpins* division differed only in detail. Each school also appears to have been allocated a number of 'General Duties' soldiers from each of the Territorial infantry regiments in the Corps. These were men over-age for front line service. Each of the *Chasseur* divisions had a battalion of four large (400 officers and men) companies of Territorial light infantry for support and administrative tasks; some of these appear to have been used in the mountain warfare school at Caprino.

On 28 January 1918 four British officers, selected by their divisional commanders to attend a *Cours Superieur d'Infanterie*, for *Chefs de Bataillons et Commandants de Compagnies*, arrived at Garda. The 7th Division nominee was Lieutenant Colonel Richard Nugent O'Connor DSO MC, a Regular Army officer of the Cameronians (Scottish Rifles), at that time commanding 2/1 HAC, and in another war to become famous for his bold exploits in the deserts of North Africa. The 48th Division selectee was Captain GH Greenwell, a company commander in the 1/4 Oxfordshire & Buckinghamshire Light Infantry. Tuition was conducted entirely in French and was described by Captain Greenwell as interesting, and the work not too hard; the hours more than acceptable after front line service in France or Flanders. The working day started at 8 am with a lecture and discussion which lasted until 10 am; return to the mess for *déjeuner* at 11 am, recommence at 2 pm, for either another lecture and discussion, or a demonstration; equitation between 2.30 pm and 5.30 pm, and an occasional evening or night session, sometimes out of doors. The demonstrations included displays of firepower, including artillery and medium machine gun barrages, infantry-artillery co-operation in the deliberate attack, with weapons firing live ammunition, including rifle and hand

Captain Greenwell.
Archive OBLI

78

grenades, mortars and small arms. The accommodation, in another resort, Punta San Vigilio, was excellent, and the course was apparently enjoyed by all concerned. Captain Greenwell noted that everyone, students and staff, were on the best of terms.

Sadly, no remnants of the two French schools have been located at Garda or Caprino, although a café owner in the latter could recall his parents, now deceased, talking about the *Alpini Francesi.*

An itinerary for a mini-tour covering the sites of the French schools, Rovereto Museum and Matarello CWGC graves is at the end of the guide, as Tour M.

British Schools

GHQ Central Schools were established near Torreglia, in the *Colli Euganei*, a cluster of sugar-loaf hills southwest of Padua. The hills have beautiful scenery and in 1918 was a popular holiday area, with good rail, tramway and canal connections to Padua.

The Schools occupied an area, *about six and half* [miles] *long and generally about two miles wide*, to quote one account, in the northeast corner of the hills. RQMS Corbett: .... *A range of plutonic hills near.... It was a lovely place with rich soil, fine trees, and the priceless boon of plenteous water-springs.*

The **Army Wing** ran courses for potential company and platoon commanders, company sergeant majors and platoon sergeants, based on a Second Army syllabus. Part of the syllabus dealt with hill-fighting, based on both *Alpini* and North-West Frontier experience. Infantry battalions were required to send one company to this course, partly to learn the techniques of hill-fighting, and partly to act as demonstrators and servants/actors for the company staff course.

The **Artillery School** trained officers and senior NCOs for field and siege (howitzer) batteries, and also ran a Trench Mortar School, with courses on the 6" Newton Mobile, and 3" Stokes, mortars.

The **Gas School** provided refresher training for personnel attending all school courses, including pack transport personnel (mules liked to eat one type of horse gas mask, and were allegedly impervious to some

Colli Euganei.

RFA Field Battery in training, Italy, Spring 1918. Peter Grudgings

gases). This school also carried out experimental work, for example, in relation to operations on the Asiago plateau, devising gas-proof door-seals for dug-outs blown from solid rock, and disposing of Austrian gas shells and bombs.

This school also tested the use of smoke to mask movement in mountain valleys. This was demonstrated at Torreglia before an audience of high-and middle-ranking officers of various armies. Nothing seems to have come of this interesting idea, thought up by Lieutenant Colonel Lesley John Barley DSO RE. He was a specialist Gas Officer in the Second Army and accompanied General Plumer to Italy. He helped the Italians improve anti-gas techniques, which had been found wanting during the early stages of Caporetto, and ordered for them, without authority, 800,000 British gas masks. Fortunately the Italian government paid without demur.

The **Musketry School** trained subalterns as Range Control Officers,

No 3 Platoon, A Company, 1/4 Oxf & Bucks LI, Torreglia, September 1918; Platoon Cmdr, 2/Lt WRB Brooks, seated second right. Archive OBLI

NCOs as unit small arms instructors, or as instructors for brigade (later divisional) medium machine-gun units. Some ranges were laid out with the targets well above, or below, the level of the firing point, to practise students in the problems of firing up and downhill. The school also administered the School of Sniping which trained infantry battalion Scouts, brigade or divisional Observers, and anti-aircraft Observers. It also provided training in sniping for selected infantrymen, some of whom also attended the basic course. The School adopted and adapted a programme developed on the Western Front at the First Army School of Sniping, Observation and Scouting. That school had been developed by Major A Hesketh-Prichard DSO MC. It was established in 1916 under the patronage of Lieutenant General Sir Richard Haking, GOC XI Corps, who provided support and encouragement. He imported his enthusiasm for 'S.O.S.' to Italy, and found that his fellow corps commander, the Earl of Cavan and General Plumer held similar views. The Italian mountain terrain was ideal for the work of long-range observers, who also relished the vistas obtained from the Montello. The width and undulating terrain of No Man's Land on the Asiago Plateau provided many opportunities for battalion Scouts.

The **Signalling School** provided a variety of courses, from elementary field signalling to training instructors for infantry and artillery units, wireless operators for division-brigade links, and operators and equipment mechanics for airborne artillery fire control links. The school covered every technique of signalling/communications used by the BEF including: field and airline (wire) telephony; transmission of Morse code by light and sound; use of signal flags (Semaphore); power buzzers (by which Morse code passed using the earth as the transmission medium); wireless telegraphy; and some aspects of the care and handling of carrier pigeons and messenger dogs.

The **Pack Transport Demonstration School** trained unit transport personnel in the handling and loading of mules. This included having handlers practise harnessing, making-up loads, and unloading while wearing dark glasses, and unharnessing mules blindfold. The handlers were also taught to avoid bulky loads, especially if using some of the Italian tracks near the top of the escarpment below the British divisional base at Carriola, adjacent to Bydand Corner, as

Mule train in the mountains

British infantry returning from field training, GHQ Schools, Torreglia. Summer 1918. IWM Q26469

mules were obviously unable to judge the width of their loads.

The **Camouflage School** taught all aspects of concealment for ground and air observation.

(There were also two billeting areas, each holding one infantry battalion, at Galzignano and Torreglia, and an out-station on top of a ridge at Rua.)

The **Central Schools**, as a branch of GHQ, also assisted staff and formation specialists (eg Divisional CRAs – Commanders, Royal Artillery) in developing tactical doctrine to meet special circumstances found in Italy. Examples include hill fighting, with publication of **SS 657 NOTES ON THE TRAINING OF INFANTRY IN HILL WARFARE**, with a short course for officers, and experiments with Yukon packs (sort of A-Frames, an idea still being touted, possibly

Newton 6" Mobile Mortar in firing position.

with the same kit, and still unpopular, in the 1970s). Another example was *SS 668 PACK TRANSPORT*, covering what appears to be everything on the subject, from information about the use of Italian saddlery if issued to British units, through notes and illustrations of loads such as corrugated iron, bed blankets, hay, boxes of hand grenades, trench boards and soldiers' large packs (a mule could carry 12), to competitions for handlers to stimulate interest and technical competence.

Other developments in which the Central Schools had a role appear to have been training methods and material for the 6" Newton Mobile Mortar for use in both mountains and open warfare. *SS 670 THE 6" MOBILE MORTAR* contained all the information needed to assemble, move across country by mule, handle in action, strip, clean, adjust and repair one or several of these fearsome weapons (the barrel was in two halves; there was no sight, the base-plate consisted of several blocks of wood, bolted together). The maximum range, with Charge 5, was about 1,400 yards. If handled efficiently it was a useful 'force-multiplier' in defence, or in a set-piece attack, but it allegedly had a tendency to blow-up after about sixty rounds. There is a 6" Newton Mobile Mortar on display in the *Museo Storico Italiano Della Guerra, Rovereto;* see Tour M.

TOUR E
Brenta Plain, Padua CWGC Sites, Colli Euganei

Start: A4/A31 junction.
Map: LAC Padova. (A very good 1:25,000 map of the school sites can be found in PRO WO369/190, it is an invaluable aid to exploring the hills).
Itinerary: Leave the A4 at the Vicenza Est junction. Immediately after the toll-booth turn right for Torri di Quartesolo then right again at the **SS11**, then second left (at traffic lights) for Grumolo delle Abadesse.

Irrigation ditch, of the type leapt across by the 1/8 Worcestershire Regiment, winter 1917/18. FM

Note along the way the irrigation channels, subjects of controversy between the Italian authorities and the Allied HQs as the troops used them for washing, bathing and other unsanitary functions. These fields were well-known, if not exactly popular, with British infantrymen. Hereabouts they practised open warfare. Imagine trying to jump a channel when laden with 60lbs of equipment, carrying a cold, wet and slippery rifle or Lewis gun, in the rain and being bayed at by angry NCOs! And then returning to a cold billet and a tasty meal of luke-warm bully beef stew, 'biscuits, hard, thirty-two hole' and weak tea.

Follow the road under the railway, and then turn right and drive for 2 km to traffic lights. Turn right and continue until a piazza and a war memorial will appear on the right; there is usually parking space in the square. The memorial is flanked by four unusual weapons, Austrian 12 cm pneumatic mortars. These strange devices were virtually silent in operation and easy to operate; a well-trained crew could fire about one round every two minutes. The weapons were powered by compressed air, stored in steel cylinders with a capacity of 20 litres, sufficient for 10-11 shots. The cylinders were recharged by steam-powered compressors, standard issue in mountainous or stony areas for rock-drilling units. These very rare and interesting weapons, a tribute to the ingenuity of the Austro-Hungarian armaments industry, are worth a small detour.

Leave the square and turn left, go to the traffic lights at the end of the main street, and turn right to rejoin the road from Torri di Quartesolo.

Villa Contarini and antique fair, Piazzola Sul Brenta. FM

Austro-Hungarian Pneumatic mortars, Grumolo delle Abadesse. FM

Drive into Camisano Vicentino, another billeting area for British troops, but nothing much seems to have been written about it; even that diligent diarist RQMS Corbett merely noted that;

> ...after a long march we stopped next night at a hamlet about
> two miles beyond Camisano (a nice little town)...

and follow the signs for Piazzola sulle Brenta.

In 1917 Piazzola was a rural community but is now a suburb of Vicenza and Padua. Around the time of the Great War two railways ran through the town, each with its own station. The lines crossed at right angles on the southern edge of the built-up area; the east-west line ran from the main Vicenza-Padua line near Grumolo, and crossed the river Brenta to join a north-south line linking Padua and Bassano del Grappa. The north-south line through Piazzola was a private one financed by a local entrepreneur to remove shingle extracted from the Brenta. The line ran north to the Vicenza-Cittadella line at Ospitale di Brenta and was used in 1918 by British supply trains.

The main attraction of Piazzola is an enormous villa with a very wide frontage, the Villa Contarini, at the side of the main square. The villa was used as a combined billet and HQ by the British during the winter of 1917/18, and was recalled as being bitterly cold, as there was no wood for heating the huge rooms. The town hosts an antique fair on the last Sunday of each month, there are good selections of militaria and some postcard stalls, one of the latter run in recent years by a lady from Lancashire; very useful for those without much Italian.

More CWGC Graves

The next stop is the CWGC Great War plot in the Padua Municipal Cemetery; the following short detour takes in a solitary CWGC grave in a village cemetery, that of a Private soldier of the Royal Warwickshire Regiment.

From Piazzola find signposts, on the south side of the town, for

Padua Municipal Cemetery, December 1999, CWGC plot. FM

Villafranca Padovana, and drive until a small clover-leaf junction appears, the start of a recently built by-pass. Ignore the by-pass and drive straight on into the town to a crossroads, turn right and then left into the Via dell Rimembrenza; the *Cimitero Communale* is at the bottom, on the left, and the grave is on the right, towards the south wall. The grave is marked by standard CWGC headstone, indicating the last resting place of 203553 Private R. McLachlan, 2/Royal Warwickshire, of Glasgow and Coventry, who died of sickness on 3 March 1918, 37 years of age. The battalion was one of two Regular army ones in 22 Brigade, 7th Division (the other was 1/R.Welsh Fusiliers) along with a Kitchener battalion, 20th Manchesters, and a Territorial Force one of the 2/1 HAC. In February 1918 the Division was on the Montello, and late on the 24th the GOC, General TH Shoubridge, was advised it was to return to France as part of XI corps, along with the 5th Division. By 2 March the Division had withdrawn from the Montello. Advance parties had departed for France and the main force was about to entrain west of Padua, between Piazzola and Montegaldella on the Bacchiglione river. At some time during the following day Private McLachlan breathed his last and was buried in the cemetery at Villafranca, at that time a tiny crossroads community serving a farming area famous for rice growing. The next morning the Battalion marched off to the station and started to entrain for France. But they were reprieved from returning to the mud of France and Flanders; later that day, 4 March, and when some men were, to quote the OH, *already seated in their train* i.e. squatting uncomfortably in groups of *Hommes 40*, the move was cancelled. The 41st Division went to France instead, along with the 5th and Corps troops from XI Corps.

The grave of Pte McLachlan lay unvisited by anyone but CWGC staff for possibly eighty years, until two ex-members of what had once been the Royal Warwickshire Regiment visited the site while serving as mobilised reservists in northern Italy during NATO operations in the Balkans. Oddly, as of February 2002, the name of Pte R McLachlan did not appear on the CWGC website.

The next stop is the CWGC Plot in the Padua Municipal Cemetery. From Villafranca drive south towards Padua. After about 7 km the road passes under the A4 autostrada and immediately after the bridge bear right for *Villaguattera*, and once there take the **left** turn off the main road where it bears right just beyond the centre of the village, pass under a railway line and head towards the **SS11** and Padua. At the **SS11**, turn **left**, and drive towards Padua. Ignore for the moment a CWGC sign pointing to the left about 1 km from the turn onto the **SS11**; that is for a Second World War site. Continue along the main road until it becomes a fly-over crossing a dual carriageway by-pass. The Municipal Cemetery is on the left, tucked into the corner of the 'off' ramp and the dual carriageway; it has a red and white banded brick wall with some odd-looking gate towers. There is plenty of parking space in front of the cemetery. Go through the main entrance and turn right; the CWGC plot is on the left, on the corner. It contains twenty-five graves, fourteen of men who died of wounds or disease in No 37 Casualty Clearing Station, Padua, in the winter of 1917/18. Some of the graves are of aircrew based at airfields north of Padua and killed in action during the battle to establish Allied air supremacy along the Piave. Buried here is Major Robert Gregory, MC, Chevalier of the Legion of Honour, 4/Connaught Rangers, attached to 66 Squadron RFC, killed in action on 23 January 1918, and commemorated anonymously in Yeat's poem, *An Irish Airman Foresees His Death*. Three of the graves are for men killed in late December 1917 during German air raids. In November 1917 the Germans transferred a squadron of Gotha GIV bombers from Ypres to Pordenone, north-east of Venice, to put more pressure onto the Italians. The squadron was tasked with bombing, by night, cities west of the Piaves or, to be precise, Allied command centres and logistics nodes in Treviso, Castelfranco, Cittadella, Padua and Vicenza. Venice was also to be bombed but, apparently, that was prevented through the personal intercession (again) of Empress Zita of Austria with Kaiser Wilhelm. In a raid on the night of 28 December two subalterns of 1/Dorset were killed while walking home to their billets: Second Lieutenants Alec Leslie Hill, of Exeter, and Charles Willis Roberts, 28 years old, a

Padua Municipal Cemetery; December 1917: burial of three British soldiers killed during German air-raids. Taylor Collection.

married man from Hampshire. The bombers returned the following night, and claimed another British victim, Corporal Albert Sidney Vincent, Army Service Corps, attached HQ Second Army, and a native of Norwich. All three men were buried in the Municipal Cemetery with full military honours at a service attended by British and French officers and men, and Italian military, civil and religious dignitaries.

After the war eleven bodies were brought in from a small community cemetery at Abano Bagni (now Abano Terme) in the *Colli Euganei*, the next stop on this tour.

GHQ Schools

Leave the Municipal Cemetery, and return along the **SS11**, past the road to the CWGC Second World War Cemetery, mainly devoted to Allied aircrew, but with the graves of some South African troops of all races. (Worth a visit; a short drive down the road, on the right hand side.) and join the **SS250** for Abano Terme. After 1.5 km the main road swings left; carry straight on to San Biagio. After 1 km a road on the left leads to the Abbazia di Praglia, in 1918 occupied by the Army Wing. The buildings on the right opposite this road were occupied by the Commandant, Central Schools, and his staff, but the present inhabitants of the properties round about have only vague recollection

GHQ Schools; Abbey at Torreglia

that the *Inglesi* were here.

The only relics of the British Army Schools in the *Colli Euganei* located by the author are some enigmatic craters in a small valley west of Teolo, the site of the Trench Mortar Range. A local farmer stated that over the years a number of *bomba* had been uncovered in the course of ploughing, but indicated that was not surprising as the Italian Army and the *Wehrmacht*, trained here during the Second World War. As there is so little left to see in the hills, rather than provide a general tour the sites of the various schools are listed below for the tourist to drive round at leisure. The *Colli Euganei* are unusual and attractive, and very popular throughout the year. The area is famous for health spas, specialising in thermal baths and the use of volcanic mud for rheumatism and muscular injuries. Norman Gladden mentions staying in a billet in this area, *our unpretentious little building had an unusual amenity in a small spring by the roadside which gave forth a constant stream of hot water, a boon for which we were extremely grateful.* Several of these are to be found to the west of the hills, or were to be found in the mid-1990s, but the owners of the properties were very protective of them, and reluctant to provide much information, fearing hordes of visitors. It appears the flow is somewhat diminished since Norman Gladden's day, but it must have been a boon to unwashed soldiers used to little better than a bucket of cold, and none-too-clean, water.

British Expeditionary Force (Italy) Central Schools

Army Wing – Abbazia di Praglia
Artillery School – Bresseo
Gas School – Bresseo
Musketry School – Luvigliano
School of Sniping – Monte Rina
Signalling School – Valsanzibio
Camouflage School – Abbazia di Praglia
Pack Transport School – Vallerega
Trench Mortar School – Teolo
Battalion billeting areas – Galzignano, Torreglia, Monte Rua

To return to the **A4 start point** from the entrance to the road to the Abbazia, **either**
a) retrace your steps to the **SS11** and follow that to a the autostrada entrance at Grisignano di Zocco, or
b) to see the area the British were initially to occupy in November

1917, and another solitary grave, turn right out of the road to the Abbazia, then immediately left, for **Saccolongo,** and from there to **Creolo** a tiny community on the bank of the river Bacchiglione. At the south end is a CWGC headstone, for Pte GW Weston, 1/Bedfords, who died on 27 March 1918. No further information has come to light. The grave was located in 1997 by the author and some colleagues using the CWGC Register **Italy 15-93 Minor Cemeteries**, and visited as part of Remembrance Day activities. *Nil Oblivscarus.*

From Creola return to Saccolongo, and follow the signs for *Montegaldella*, a fine town with a fascinating crenellated wall, with a twin, *Montegalda*, across the Bacchiglione. Gladden passed through the town in November 1917, but only records that bread was unobtainable, and that all he and his colleagues could buy to eat were some dried figs. The British were supposed to have occupied a line of defences along the south bank of the Bacchiglione river, but instead moved to the Montello.

From Montegalda it is only 5kms to the A4 entrance at Grisignano.

Tour F
Valli dell'Agno, Orange Line, Malo Di Monte

Introduction

When XIV (Br) Corps deployed onto the Asiago Plateau in March 1918 two divisions were always in the line with the third in reserve near Vicenza. The equivalent of at least one brigade was kept occupied in the Central School described above, while the remainder were stationed in a Reserve Area in the Valle dell'Agno, west of Vicenza.

The Leoncino Inn, Tavernalle, 1918.

The British occupied several villages at the southern end of the valley, and a number of French support units, and infantry and artillery units enjoying a break from frontline duties, were in hamlets in the middle reaches. While the upper section, from Valdagno to Recoara, was devoted to Italian Army supply dumps and service units supporting operations on the M. Pasubio *massif*. This tour takes the tourist from the west end of Vicenza along the road used by British troops when travelling by steam tram to or from the city on official or unofficial journeys, into and through parts of the Valle dell'Agno and over the *Colli Vicentini* by the road along which they marched to and from the Asiago Plateau.

Start: A4/A31 Autostrada interchange.

Maps: LAC **Vicenza**; there is a useful map of the training grounds and ranges in WO369/189

Itinerary: Drive towards the **Vicenza Ouest** (West) exit and join the **SS11** west bound for Alte, and Verona. The **SS11** for the next few kilometres is busy and traffic can be slow, but a letter home in 1918 also complained about congestion on the road between Vicenza and the 'Valley Danno' ....

The Leoncino Inn, Tavernalle, 1998. FM

Drive for 6 km to Tavernalle and look for signs indicating *Sovvizo* to the right; turn right at the traffic lights and take the first road left and up to a small carpark by a war memorial. There is a small but well-stocked supermarket by the carpark, handy for picnic supplies. A short stroll around the area by the traffic lights reveals the Albergo Leoncino, little changed from 1918 when it housed the British Town Major, and his opposite number, the Italian *Commando di Tappa,* and billets for a brigade HQ from one or other of the division in reserve in the Valle dell'Agno. There was also a small detachment of British, French and Italian ammunition experts billeted here, to supervise large dumps of artillery shells, bombs and grenades further along the **SS11**, just beyond the railway goods yard. A store for gun charges lay on the other side of the station, too close to the Leoncino for some people's comfort as most of the sentries persisted in smoking even when the unloading or loading took place. Close to the Leoncino, exact location unclear but thought to be in the disused tramway station (by the traffic lights), was an Expeditionary Forces Canteen (EFC) Wholesale and Retail Canteen which supplied a wide range of tinned foods, sauces, condiments, bottled soft drinks and cordials, confectionery, tobacco, stationery, boot polish, etc to unit canteens and individuals, including passing French and Italian soldiers.

From the car park return to the traffic lights, turn into the road bearing half-right, for Montecchio Maggiore.

This was the original line of the steam tramway/road-railway mentioned above, but it was realigned in the 1920s to follow the **SS11** before swinging back up into the Valle dell'Agno. After a couple of kilometres, once out of the suburbs of Tavernalle, a ridge appears at three o'clock, crowned by two castles.

These, according to some local sources, are the inspiration of Shakespeare's *Romeo and Juliet*, Montecchio being Montague/Montacute in another form. Be that as it may, the castle on the left is allegedly that of Juliet's, the one on the right Romeo's. They were very popular with British troops in the summer of 1918, when they would make their way up to the airy heights for an evening stroll, to catch the cool breeze and hear the Alpine Swifts screaming as they swooped around the castle towers.

Montecchio Maggiore was one of several British billeting areas

The two castles, Montecchio Maggiore. Comune di Montecchio Maggiore

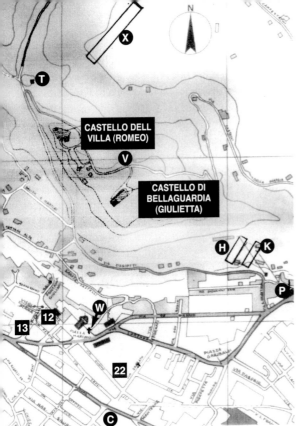

MONTECCHIO MAGGIORE

X. **X Range** (200yds: 8 Targets)
T. **Tower/Gate for X Range**
V. **Viewpoint**
H. **H Range** (75yds. 6 Targets)
K. **K Range** (75yds. 8 Targets)
P. **Parrochiale** (Church)
W. **War Memorial**
B. **Baths**
C. **Cemetery**

Training Areas: 13, 22, 12

Grid 1km

Montecchio Maggiore.

within the valley. It held one brigade, with another stationed at
Chiampo and the third in other villages further up the valley. GHQ
BEF(I) established an outpost of the Central Schools here, and built
twenty-two ranges and the same number of training areas in the lower
valley between Montecchio Maggiore and Cornedo, some five
kilometres south of Valdagno. Some were on the ridge below Juliet's
castle. One, an elementary field firing range, was in a small valley,
Campestrini, on the north-east flank of the ridge.

Drive into Montecchio Maggiore, along the Via Lombardi which
becomes the Corso Mateotti as it passes a large church, the Parrochiale
di San Pietro. At the traffic lights turn right into, the Via San Valentino
(there should be signs for *il castello Giulietta*) and round to the left.
Stop after 450m. Immediately on the right was the firing point of H
Range and about 100m down hill was K Range, for eight firers. The
butts were above the Parrochiale, in an old quarry. Drive on up the hill
to a hairpin bend; park on the wide verge. Look to the left, out over the

Privates three: John MacLennan, right, Italy, 1918. Katriona Coutts collection

valley. Training Area No 14 was below, on the floor of the valley, in an area now covered with housing and light industry. Close against the hillside on the left of the ridge was the tiny community of Valle where the British had use of baths in a lunatic asylum.

In 1918 the road from Montecchio Maggiore ran over the ridge and down to a large farm at Campestrini; there was no road to the castles, only a footpath from the Parrochiale.

The old road can still be followed to Campestrini/X Range. At various times between 1993 and 2001 the track was cleared of vegetation, depending on the needs of the farmer. In 1998 the farm seems to have changed hands, and the new owner modernized the buildings and improved the fields and vineyard, and may have allowed the path to again become overgrown as it led straight into his backyard.

Looking east from the hairpin bend a small tower can be seen in the remains of an orchard-cum-small holding, one of several on the eastern slope of the ridge. Some are worked as 'hobby gardens' by families from Montecchio Maggiore and Vicenza. According to one family, whom the author met while exploring the ridge (the children were pleased to demonstrate their English) the tower had been occupied by *inglesi* in the Great War, and also after the Second World War. At a guess the tower was used in 1918 as a guard post, controlling access to X Range. The targets were on the hillside below the tower, and the danger area on the right side of the range would have included the track. The range could accommodate eight firers, and had two firing points, 100 and 200 yards, described charmingly on the WO map as *Actually about 115 and 175 yards*. There is not much to see, but it is a pleasant walk down to a discrete distance from the

Range Tower, near Romeo's Castle. FM

94

farm. In many parts of the Veneto the phrase *'Inglesi; grande guerra mondiale'* seems to explain everything if challenged.

One Scottish soldier recalled the long haul up the hill from Montecchio Maggiore in letters to his family. S43554 Private John MacLennan originally enlisted in the Cameron Highlanders, and carried out his basic training at Invergordon. He arrived in France on 25 June 1916 expecting to join 6/Camerons, but was instead posted to 2/Gordons on 10 July, and wounded a few weeks later. He went with the Gordons to Italy, where he qualified as a signaller and served in the Signal Platoon. John wrote regularly to his family in Inverness, and many of his letters and postcards survive (as does his kilt). In December 1918 he was still serving in Italy, and still marveling at having survived the Western Front, the Asiago Plateau the crossing of the Piave and the advance to the Tagliamento. On 17 December 1918 he wrote to his father Sandy, a railway surfaceman at Clachnaharry, west of Inverness, in a letter headed

The Annual Magazine.

Since censorship is now not so strict, I'll be able to let you know and see for yourself if you've a map of Italy whereabouts I hang out in Sunny Italy...The village where we used to come on rest from the mountains is Montecchio [Maggiore]...*with two castles which overlook the town were* [sic] *the abode of Romeo and Juliet. The castles or their ruins stand on a high hill which we used to climb everyday for practice, and if they were as fed up of climbing it as we were no wonder they died of a broken heart.*

The ridge was one of several sites in the *Valle dell'Agno* used to soldiers in hill fighting, and to exercise their muscles for the long hikes up to the Asiago Plateau. The Gordons, like many other battalions, also marched up the hill to the tower and down Campestrini, usually in the early morning when the sun was not shining onto the road, or into the shooters' eyes.

A short drive from the bend leads to Romeo's castle; there is a fine memorial to the local regiment of *Alpini*, and a small chapel, by the castle car park. Further up the road there is another car park, at a re-cycling point 'V' on the map, from where there is a good view of the Campestrini valley and the surrounding hills, all climbed at some stage in the summer of 1918 by British soldiers. There is another car park further up for Juliet's castle, now a pleasant restaurant. Unless there is a wedding reception underway the proprietors in the past have been happy for casual visitors to explore the battlements and enjoy the views. Inside the castle there is a minor mystery: a stairway lined with

Romeo's Castle, Campestrini: site of X-Range and hills used for mountain warfare training. FM

old shutters on which are painted coats of arms. Some are of local families, such as Gonzaga (of Spanish extraction), but others are of English towns, including Canterbury, Chatham and Newcastle-under-Lyme. In the 1990s the proprietors and their staff could shed no light on this mystery.

To continue the tour, return to the traffic lights and turn right along the Via de Gasperi. There is an interesting Italian War Memorial in the Piazza Marconi, in front of the Duomo (cathedral) with names from both world wars and the 1910-1912 war in Libya. One inscription records the name of sergeant major *dispersi* [missing] *in Jugoslavia*, without a date.

Another short detour leads to the community cemetery, site of two CWGC graves. From the Piazza, turn right and drive up to a junction with a main road, the **SS246**. Turn left (it is a very busy junction) and look for the fourth large road (not track) on the right, the Via Conti Gualdo; drive down it and after a few metres turn left into the Via Cavour, then right into an unnamed (as of 2001) road for the cemetery.

Montecchio Maggiore war memorial. FM

The British graves are in the old section; through the main gate, turn right, right again into the old section, walk to the back wall, and turn left. The CWGC graves are on the left, about half way along. Staff Serjeant Ernest Reason, 25th Field Bakery, Royal Army Service Corps, died of accidental

Montecchio Maggiore Cemetery: CWGC graves. FM

injuries, 14 January 1919, when the area around was being used as a concentration area for British troops awaiting repatriation, engaged in battlefield clearance of the British sector on the Asiago Plateau, or in support of British detachments in Austria and the new state of Jugoslavia. The journey to the Channel coast took at least five days, and the soldiers were supplied with one large loaf per day of the journey, and as much as they could scrounge to barter for cheese or fruit at stations or halts along the way. Also buried here is Private Joseph Styles, 1/6 Worcesters, died 11 April 1918, age 42, another mature private soldier for whom perhaps the toil of front line service proved too much. The community cemetery is very well cared for by a small but hard-working staff. In 1995 it came as a surprise to the recently-appointed young custodian to learn that there were English graves in his charge. He contacted his predecessor who appeared on the scene very promptly, as the author and his wife were the first British visitors in living memory. He was a mine of information about the cemetery and the area around, and explained that there had indeed been sixty-seven French graves in the old section, according to the records and as quoted in the CWGC register (Site 92), apparently victims of influenza, *il spagnole* as it was called by the Italians in 1918-1920 there was something of a debate before the bodies were removed and he did not know whether they were immured at Pederobba or repatriated to France. The Italian custodians of the civil cemeteries sites with CWGC graves are invariably fascinated by British visitors and go out of their way to help. The background of the Earl Haig poppies takes some explaining, but always catches the imagination of the locals. Incidentally, the CWGC graves visited by the

Trìssino and the Valle dell'Agno; snow covered M. Pasubio massif in background. FM

Trìssino: British Army football match. Worcestershire Regt

author in community cemeteries were without exception well-maintained.

The next stop is Trìssino, in 1918 the billeting site for divisional HQs. From Montecchio Maggiore cemetery car park return to the **SS246**, turn left and drive up the valley to, and through, Ghisa: then follow the road signs through a large interchange. As the road approaches Trìssino it crosses the river Agno, and over fields used by British soldiers for football and foot drill. On 3 September 1918 it was the scene of the 7th Division Horse Show. This was a serious occasion, with not just dressage and show-jumping, but competitions for the smartest water cart and team, or ambulance, or limbers, as well as sports and other competitions where individuals and teams drawn from every unit in the division competed for prizes, and the honour of having the best 'rig' in class. General Cavan presented the prizes, and the grandstand was filled with officers from the allied nations, and a sprinkling of civilians, including women and children, all done up in their best.

Continue into the town, and find the route to the top of the hill by finding and following signs for either the Villa Trìssino Marzotto, or the Trattoria Campanile, and drive up to the car park past the (very) large church. The Villa, or villas, as there are two within the estate: the *Villa Trìssino del Ramo Baston* (the upper one) and the *Villa Trìssino Reale* ('Marzotto' was the name of the owner c.1998), were used to house the Divisional HQ offices and Officers Mess, and was

Trìssino: 7th Division Horse show, the Officer's Military Equitation class.
IWM Q

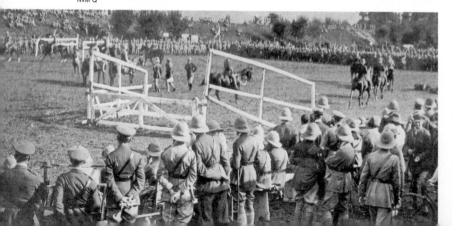

connected to the outlying brigade HQs by telephone and a system of signal lamps to provide training for signallers in sending and reading Morse code. On one occasion a senior staff officer of 48th Division caused havoc by sending incomprehensible messages, thought by the operators to be in cypher. But he was *with the drink taken*, as they say, and speedily removed from the signal station. The villa has large and ornate gardens with hundreds of statues and many ornate iron gates,

Trìssino: Villa Marzotto; Divisional HQ and Officer's Mess. FM

and some splendid views of the valley. It is open to the public but check with the Vicenza tourist board for hours of opening for at one time admission appeared to be by guided tour only.

The *Trattoria Campanile* is a pleasant spot for lunch, or even a *cappuccino* or two, and has, or had in the late 1990s, a garden which attracted numbers of Hoopoes, handsome pink and brown birds with curved beaks and a Mohican haircut.

The tour now traverses the hills to the east of the Valle dell'Agno, re-tracing the route followed by the British on their three-day march to or from the Asiago Plateau. (In summer months they marched by night to avoid the heat, and to keep the roads clear for day-time traffic.)

Return to the bridge over the Agno, and turn left immediately, then right, and left at the T-junction onto the **SS246**, and follow the signs for Castelgomberto. In 1918 this little town was the site of an Italian airfield. At least one British divisional review was enlivened by pilots performing aerobatics just above the serried ranks of unappreciative soldiers. A little later, on 21 May 1918, an Italian Savioa SP2 two-seat aircraft crashed on the airfield, killing the pilot, *Sotto Teniente* Lorenzo

Castelgomberto: Funeral of Lt Cassola & Captain Scarioni. Famiglia Gianni Tonelli, Castelgomberto

Malo: view of the Asiago Plateau, Carriola base on the left skyline.
Comune di Malo

Marchese [Marquis] Cassola, and the observer, *Capitano* Francesco Giuseppe Filippo Gianfranco Scarioni, in pre-war days a well-known sports journalist in Milan They were buried with full military honours a few days later (sources differ as to the exact date), after a solemn mass in the huge Church of Saints Peter and Paul in Castelgomberto, attended by Italian, French and British officers. The cortege was escorted by an Italian Guard of honour and a British quarter-guard and band. (Italian aircrew supposedly claimed SP2 meant *Sepolcro Per Due*; s pulchre/coffin for two.) The road from Trìssino skirts the site of the airfield, it was on the right where the road for Castelgomberto turns off the **SS246**. Continue up the **SS246**, by-passing Castelgomberto, and just beyond a road going left for Brogliano, look for a sign pointing right for Malo, and head over the hills, thankful not to be marching over them with 60 lbs of kit on your shoulders.

At the summit a side road leads to Monte di Malo, where there are some interesting remnants of a Great War reserve line of defences, concrete dug-outs and a pill box. In November 1917 the French were to occupy the Orange Line (or 'Vicenza Line') from the Monte di Malo – Malo road southwards to Vicenza, and the British from there to near Padua, along the Bacchiglione. Only one French advance party reached there, before being withdrawn and sent to M. Tomba.

The views of the escarpment from the summit and other points on this road on a clear day are excellent, and it is an easy run over to Malo; a tribute to the Italian engineers and road builders of years gone by.

In 1917-18 Malo was used by the French as a billeting area and site

Monte Cimone area: site of k.u.k. 15.2 cm long-range artillery, looking west from the Asiago Plateau. FM

French Chasseurs Alpin Band. Famiglia Gianni Tonelli, Castelgomberto

of a divisional HQ. On 12 November 1`17 the first French soldier to be seen in Malo since Napoleon's days entered the town General Levi, GOC 46th Division, *Chasseurs Alpins*, was driven through the streets in a large grey car on his way to Schio to attend a conference. That information comes from a careful diary kept by Dom Tarcisio Raumer the parish priest of Malo. Throughout the war he record d on a daily basis not just military events in the world at large but also the comings and goings of troops through, in and around his town. He noted the passage of General Ferdinand Foch, and on the 16 November that of a French General of Artillery, probably General Liset, later killed in the German air raid on Castelfranco. On the same day Dom Saumer noted that *Thiene* (important railway centre and loc tion of various Italian HQs) *and Villaverla airfield were bombarded by Austrian artillery.* These were probably 15.2 cm Long Range Sie e guns, located in the vicinity of M. Cimone (4,000 ft high) and firing at near their maximum range of 22,000 metres, but making very good shooting

On 17 November the 22nd Regiment of *Chasseurs Alpins*, Savoyards, under the command of a Major Olivier, marched into Malo behind their band. They were welcomed by military, civic and church dignitaries. Later that day *Capitaine* Dom Chevrier of Annecy, the most senior of the four padres in the regio ert, called on Dom Saumer at the presbytery. Like doctors, dentists and vets, padres, especially Roman Catholic ones, had bonds tran cending nationality, and searched out their professional colleagues wherever, and whenever, opportunity arose.

Over the next few days French cavalry patrols recce'd the roads over

French supply carts in Malo, summer, 1918. Comune di Malo

the hills, and crossing the plain to Thiene. They sometimes accompanied an Italian squadron, which was rounding up *sbandati* (drifters), stragglers from the retreat from Caporetto. In the evenings the French *Chasseurs Alpin* band gave a concert in the piazza. And so the diary goes on, including references to British troops establishing a wireless station in a field north of the town in April 1918, probably a radio-relay station to link the Divisional HQ at Trissino with Corps HQ on the Asiago Plateau, or as part of the little unknown British SIGINT (Signals Intelligence) operations.

From Malo the tourist can head for the A31 Autostrada, joining it at Thienne (follow the signs from Malo), or proceed to the next tour, which covers parts of the Asiago Plateau, but finishes on the lowlands near Malo, at the CWGC cemeteries at Dueville and Montecchio Precalcino.

TOUR G
Asiago Plateau, Foothill Sites, Cavaletto, Carriola Base

Start: A4/A31 junction.
Map: LAC **Vicenza.**
Itinerary: Head north for the mountains on the A31, leave the autostrada at the **Thiene exit** and at the main road in front of the toll booth, turn right for Marostica and Bassano del Grappa. After 5 km start looking for a sign pointing to the left for Sarcedo, turn off and at the crossroads (1 km) turn right, cross the river *(Torrente)* Astico, and then turn left for Fara Vicentino, and from there to Lonedo, once the site of GHQ/XIV Corps HQ, housed in the palatial (literally) surroundings of the Villa Godi Malinverni, where the Prince of Wales, serving as a Staff Officer at GHQ, recorded that he and his fellow officers rigged up a badminton court in a large room, possibly a ballroom, and found the game a useful diversion from what was otherwise a boring existence.

From Lonedo follow the signs for Lugo di Vicenza, and from there to Calvene, and the road up (well, across) the escarpment to Tattenham Corner, Granezza and Asiago. Calvene was the site of several British and Italian support elements, including supply and ammunition dumps. Expeditionary Forces Canteens did a roaring trade, as did coffee stalls established by various charities, including the YMCA and the American Red Cross, to refresh soldiers of any nation.

Calvene was also the terminus for a light railway line, a branch of an extensive 60 cm Decauville (the name of the French designer and manufacturer) system originally built by the Italians to link the foothill towns with standard gauge railways at Thiene and Marsan, near Bassano del Grappa. In, (probably) 1915 the system was extended southwards to Dueville station on the Vicenza-Thiene line, and northwards to Calvene. In April 1918 the British assumed responsibility for operating the Dueville-Calvene line, using men from 109th Light Railway Operating Company, RE. The terminus in Calvene was next to the 'valley' station of a cableway running up to the plateau, so in theory the passage of supplies from the main British supply base at Genoa by standard gauge train, to Decauville train, to cable-way, was simple; but it required three working parties, all day, every day. At first these were provided by the long-suffering infantry, then by prisoners of war from the growing bag provided by trench raids. (The infantry soon got wind of this, and it was, by one account, a considerable incentive to *bring 'em back alive* from a trench raid, as that would reduce the number of fatigue parties required.)

A few years ago school children in Calvene produced a small leaflet describing the impact of the Great War on the village. In 1916 many of the population were evacuated and their houses and business premises requisitioned for use by the Italian, and later British and French, soldiers manning supply dumps, stores and workshops scattered around the village. French and Italian heavy guns were sited in the village and the blast when they were fired caused extensive damage to roofs and window shutters. More damage was caused by 'overs' from *k.u.k.* artillery firing at kite-balloon launching sites at M. Paù and Mortisa on the escarpment above the village. Prisoners of war were housed in some houses outside the village; and British, French and Italian troops everywhere there was habitable space. One or other of the various nationalities, and there were officially nineteen in the *k.u.k*, brought the dreaded *spagnole* to the village, and

Foothills, Lugo di Vicenza to Cavaletto.

the leaflet records that when the people returned to their homes they suffered grievously from influenza, as had the soldiers and their captives. There was no cure other than rest and time, and fortunately few cases were fatal. The British established a small war cemetery outside Lugo di Vicenza, and another further east at Salcedo, but it has not been possible to identify whether prisoners of war were buried in them. After the armistice the bodies were removed to Montecchio Precalcino CWGC Cemetery, which at one time housed the graves of Austrian (and American) soldiers.

Transport

The problem of hauling supplies and ammunition up the face of the escarpment was solved in a variety of ways. British lorries were unable to cope easily with the hairpin bends and over-heated during the long climb, so were replaced with Italian lorries including Fiat light trucks, driven with *brio* by Army Service Corps and regimental drivers, whose enthusiasm occasionally got the better of their skill. There were at least two cableways running up from foothill villages, and for a time these were operated by personnel from 109 LRO, Company RE. The cableway passed low over spurs and outcroppings on the escarpments, where eager hands armed with hooked poles abstracted boxes of supplies and anything else useful. The scavengers include British soldiers Alf Peacock, in the 1980s and 90s a well-known lecturer on the Great War, recounts how his father, serving with 8/KOYLI on the plateau, hooked sides of beef off cable-cars, a useful supplement to endless bully beef and pork and beans; a story corroborated to the author by a grandson of another 8/KOYLI man, Pte Thomas Arthur Giblett. Eventually the British used the cableways only for ammunition and trench stores.

Anyway, drive through Calvene, and up the winding road, in 1918 called ***Cavalletto Road*** (please note that there are fourteen hairpin bends on this stretch; safe, but nauseating to the unwary) to a T-junction at ***Mortisa***, once the site of a large Italian Army pumping station which supplied the British, French and Italian forces on the

Mountain roads, Fiat light car. Museo della Grande Guerra, Canove

plateau via an extensive system of pipelines and reservoirs, the *Impianti Idrici*. Turn left, and if the traffic allows (it is not a busy road, outside August and summer weekends), stop the car and walk over to look down on some of the ridges along which Italian-designed and British built defences of the Red, or Marginal, Line, ran; very different from the Western Front.

Back in the car, and on up the road, which gradually leaves the beech and chestnut woods which are a delight in spring, and out onto and across open pastures. This road was used by EFC Canteen lorries, travelling shops, which took a good range of groceries, confectionery and tobacco items as close to the front line as circumstances, i.e. enemy barrages, allowed. At San Sisto Ridge on the Asiago Plateau a lorry could get to within fifty yards of the support trench; but elsewhere the nearest 'sales point' was anything up to a mile behind the front line. Remains of sauce bottles, sardine tins, and cigarette cans (50s of Players) can still occasionally be unearthed on the plateau, when walking along the sides of the trenches.

At *Costa della Mare*, a tiny hamlet perched on the edge of the escarpment, there are some enigmatic concrete remains on the right side of the road just after the hairpin bend (No. 8) at the east end of the 'main street'. In April 1918 there was an RFC kite-balloon site on this spur. The KB was flown as often as the winds flowing up the escarpment allowed, and the observers had superb views well into the enemy rear area, and its supply dumps and cableway base stations. These remains housed the drive mechanism; damage or destroy that and everything stopped. The cables became unhitched from the pulleys, and it took considerable effort to repair and restore it to working order. The KBs were safe from Austrian fighters after April 1918 when the combined Italian, British and French defensive counter-air operations confined the enemy squadrons to their own airspace. But the balloons, British, French and Italian, were clearly visible and the work of their observers in directing artillery shoots was making life difficult for the *k.u.k.* in the front and support lines on the Asiago plain. Most of the KB sites were out of range of the *k.u.k.* artillery, but a few guns could reach out to the slopes around Costa della Mare, and make life interesting for the balloon handlers, and disturb the concentration of the observers bobbing far (16,000 ft) above.

EFC mobile store truck, Italy, 1918.

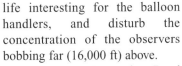

Continue up the road to Bend 12. Just over half a kilometre

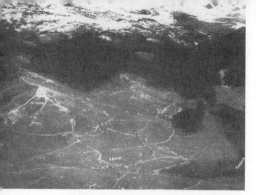

Asiago plateau, photographed from RFC Kite Balloon, Spring, 1918.

beyond this is a track, a sharp turn off to the right, into *Casa Cavalletto*, once the site of a British hutted camp, an overflow from the vast base at Granezza, a few kilometres ahead. This was a British camp, holding a battalion-sized unit (1200 men). Corbett described it as Club Camp, from Club Track, which ran from here up hill and down dale, to the junction of the Val Scaletta and Langabissa Roads south of M. Torle:

> *...some good hutments perched on top of one of the highest and least accessible peaks on the range. From this ridge, at dawn, before the mists come up, a most amazing view is had. One sees the plain of Venetia like a map, long rivers, countless villages, and towns, the great cities of Padua, and Vicenza, Venice like a fleet of ships in her lakes, the Euganei Hills islanded on the plain, the vast sheet of the Adriatic with the Dalmatian ranges beyond; and to the south the endless wall of the Apennines past San Marino and Ancona: to the visible edge of the world...a sad event: It was also a farewell feast to Serjeant A. Ashworth, our incomparable Master Cook, who left us to take a commission, and to Lulu, our beloved interpreter, who also was reft from us.*

In the mid-1990s only a few stone-built foundations for huts remained to be seen, but they also appeared to be in the process of being turned into a new outhouse for the present Casa Cavalletto. But the vistas are unchanged, although smog in recent decades has made catching sight of them problematic. One lucky chance took the author to that road early one Sunday morning in November 1994, having come off-watch and finding the day clear, cold, bright and breathless. A fast drive along deserted roads to Asiago town, then Granezza, and the road down hill past Casa Cavaletto, was the best tonic in the world, and you could see forever. It was one of those chance trips which are unforgettable. And, of course, no camera...! But the view is still there to be enjoyed, and so is the smog – sometimes.

Continue up the road, and slow down after the next (left hand) bend, as the track leading to the CWGC Cemetery. Cavaletto is about 200 metres ahead, on the right. There should be a sign on the left hand side of the road, pointing right. As of late 2001 parking was almost impossible at the road side. The rough track down to the cemetery it is not recommended for cars. Further up the road on

CWGC Cemetery Cavaletto, 1919.

the right, about half a kilometre, there is a picnic area, and space for cars; busy at summer weekends and mobbed in August, but usually empty during the week out of the high season. Alternatively, roadside parking is possible further up Cavaletto Road, at the junction with Marginal and Longdin Crescent. The road back down to the cemetery is narrow and lacks verges, so have a care. The cemetery is at the bottom of a hollow, and almost visible from the road. The Cemetery Register describes the site as a *small valley of great natural beauty*, and that describes it exactly.

The cemetery was established close to an Advanced Operating Station, described in the *Asiago, Battleground Europe Guide* and illustrated here. Briefly, before the AOS was established at Cavaletto, casualties requiring major surgery had to be transported by ambulance down the escarpment to Casualty Clearing Stations at Dueville and Montecchio Precalcino. In May 1918, after some deaths in transit, the Director of Medical Services decided to establish an Advanced Operating Station on the plateau, and the valley shown on the map at Cavaletto was selected as it was quiet, airy, secluded and out of range of much of the *k.u.k.* artillery. There was also a good supply of fresh water, from a reservoir and water distribution point supplied by a pipeline from the pumping station at Mortisa. Finally, the combe was close to the main route down the escarpment, and to roads on the plateau leading to and from various Field Ambulance sites, and their

Cavaletto, Longdin Cresent, Tattenham Corner.

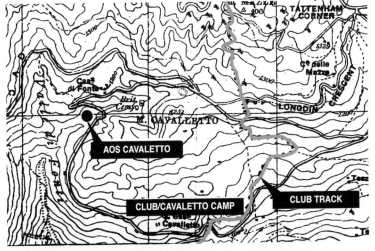

RAMC Advanced Operating Station, Cavaletto, July, 1918. IWM Q26871

Advanced Dressing Stations.

Cavaletto was one of ten war-cemeteries in the British sector, namely: Barental Road (2), M. Kaberlaba, M. Langabissa, Princes Road (also called Boscon Road cemetery), Magnaboschi (nowhere near there; it was at Valle, near Cesuna), M. Lemerle (above Magnaboschi), M. Sunio, Granezza, and Cavalletto.

Cavaletto Cemetery contains the remains of 100 British soldiers, 19 of whom were originally buried at a small war cemetery near an Advanced Dressing Station near M. Sunio, on the edge of the escarpment.

From the picnic site drive on up the road and turn left at the first junction for the next tour.

To reach Asiago, bear right at the junction, left at the next and on to what in 1918 was Tattenham Corner, and through the forest to the town.

TO MARGINAL ROAD, M. SUNIO & CARRIOLA, LONGDIN CRESENT, TATTENHAM CORNER & GRANEZZA

ALTERNATIVE SITE FOR WARD 'B'

Kitchen

6 Beds for Officers

W A R D 'B'
3 0 B E D S

N

W A R D 'A'
30 BEDS

Not to Scale

X Ray Hut

Reception Marquee

Preparation | Resuscitation | Operating Theatre

Platform

17' | 16' | 35'

Hot Water Apparatus

Dressing Store

Sterilizing Room

TO CALVE DUEVILI

6' | 14'

Proposed layout: AOStn Cavaletto.

A Field Dressing Station in the mountains on the Italian Front.

THE ASIAGO PLATEAU

Introduction

During the Great War the Marginal Road, in one form or another, ran along the edge of the escarpment from the Brenta valley to M. Paù, above the river Astico. It was a key military supply and communications route, lined with ammunition and stores dumps, hutted camps, workshops, medical facilities and cableway stations. Space on the plateau behind the Allied frontline was at a premium, so Italian, French and British support units were frequently intermingled, apparently without much rancour. The Italian officer allocating space and maintaining records of use and abuse must have been kept very busy.

The road was bordered by trenches and dug-outs, and horse and mule standings. A water pipe-line ran along much of its length, and remains are still visible in places. There were numerous incinerators for burning waste from toilets and horse lines as it could not be buried due to the shallow layer of soil covering the limestone of the plateau. Wherever you drive along this road there are ruins or remains of Great War premises, and a couple are illustrated here. The 'curved shelves' near Serona Point, caused much head scratching among the few British visitors to the area. Eventually the problem was solved by Sr Vittorio Corà of Asiago, an expert on the plateau and the battlefields. He identified them as storage sites which were being built at the time of the Armistice, and never completed. They were probably intended for stacks of boxes or ammunition, stored at the same height as the beds of carts or lorries, which would have arrived an departed in a one-way system.

The 'curved shelves', thought to be a transhipment point for rations and stores allowing the RASC to uplift and deliver.

Note: some PRO maps and modern walker's charts show a track running up to the Marginal Road from what in 1918 was Langabissa Road, which linked Handley Cross with Pria dell'Acqua. This road appears as the *Val Scaletta Road* on Great War maps. It is very rough; the author, his wife and a colleague drove up it one autumn afternoon, and it was definitely a 'tuneless whistling' ride. Be warned!

TOUR H
The Marginal Road, Carriola Base, General's Valley, Cavan Road

Start: Junction of Cavalletto Road, the Marginal Road and Longdin Crescent (which leads to Tattenham Corner.

Maps: *Altipiano di Asiago* Tourist Board Great War map [South Sheet]; LAC *Vicenza* for routes to and from the plateau.

Itinerary: At the junction, turn left and drive along the Marginal Road: rarely used outside the high season and summer weekends, and then mainly by locals and mountain bikers. (On page 142 of *Asiago* there is a note about the road being unsuitable for cars; as of 2001 there were still stretches surfaced with stones and gravel. The author has driven along it on a number of occasions in recent years; it requires care in places, but presented no problems of safety or damage to a hired car.)

Drive along the Marginal Road to M. Sunio where there is a fine example of a reservoir, a *serbatoio*, and drinking trough. On the other side of the road, and down hill, the foundations of a British Army camp are still visible, possibly part of the ADS mentioned earlier.

Continue along the road until it makes a right angle turn to the right.

Marginal Road. Cavaletto - Carriola; Reservoir and foundations of camp.

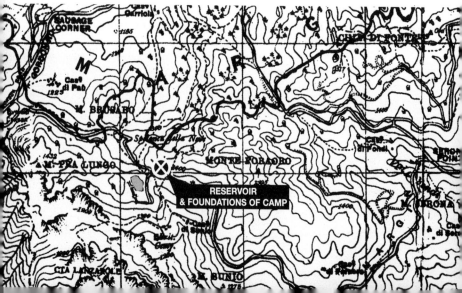

Tattenham Corner. Roger Garbett collection

The Marginal Road became Gordon Road, and on the corner a track goes off to the left, and forms a miniature race track round a large pond. At the south side of the pond the road became Bydand Corner, another relic of the Gordon Highlanders and commemorating that regiment's motto (*Bydand*: Staunch). This area is Bocchetta Paù and is worth exploring; there is plenty of parking space at the side of the tracks. The area takes its name from the summit to the west, M. Paù, once the site of an OP reached by a tunnel, and a signal station in a cave, recalled as being *safe but smelly*. The tunnel and caves on M. Paù have so far eluded the author, and may have been filled-in as a safety precaution. A short walk down Gordon Road to the south-east corner of the hollow leads to a network of footpaths along the face of the escarpment, some once used by British troops to move on foot up (or down) the escarpment between billeting areas in the foothill villages of Caltrano, Camisino and San Donna, and Carriola base.

A splendid photograph in the Imperial War Museum shows the view from a muletrack near the Bocchetta, and a copy appeared in Norman Gladdens' book *Across the Piave*. It is reproduced here to illustrate the tracks and paths up which men and mule-trains had to travel, and the height of the escarpment. To reach the photographer's viewpoint, pass out of the *Bocchetta* at Bydand Corner and

Marginal Road: Malga Fondi, 1918. Roger Garbett collection

Marginal Road: No. 2 reservoir, Monte Sunio. FM

Marginal Road: Malga Fondi. FM

Marginal Road: probable site of a Field Ambulance. FM

Monte Paù: Caltrano, looking up. 1918.

walk to the right for about 100 metres until the pillar rocks appear. But please note that the undergrowth along the escarpment grows rapidly, and the view may be obscured. The author has visited it on three occasions over five years; once with perfect visibility, once with none because of vegetation, and one fine day when sudden mist blotted out everything.

M. Paù was also the site of Kerr's Camp, named after the Commanding Officer of 2/Borders Lieutenant Colonel WW Kerr DSO MC. In July 1914 William Walton Kerr was a Company Sergeant Major with the Battalion, went to France with it in August and was

Monte Pau, Caltrano, looking down, 1998.

Monte Paù: Boccheta Paù.
Comune di Caltrano

Monte Paù: entrance to HQ dug-out. Museo della Grande Guerra, Canove

commissioned in the field shortly afterwards. In three and half years he rose through the ranks to become its commanding officer, a tribute to his outstanding ability and force of character. Lieutenant Colonel Kerr was killed in action on 3 May 1918. The Battalion, part of 20 Brigade, was manning the left forward brigade sub-sector, along the south bank of river Ghelpac. The 2/Borders were in the front line, occupying the section between Perghele Ridge and Ghelpac Fork (see *Asiago*). The Battalion Battle HQ was in a cluster of huts, dugouts and trenches behind a small hill just south of the river bed, near the Buco di Cesuna. On the night of 2/3 May a flanking battalion raided *k.u.k.* trenches at Stella, near the remains of the village of Canove, and the enemy retaliated with an artillery barrage on British positions

Lt Col William Walton Kerr, 2/Border. KIA 3 May 1918, Ghelpac Valley. Archive King's Own Border Regt

Barrack hut; Kerr's camp, Summer, 1918. Museo della Grande Guerra, Canove

Office and storage huts used by British battalions in the Ghelpac Valley, winter 1918/19 Archive OBLI

along the Ghelpac. A shell hit the hut where Lieutenant Colonel Kerr was working, killing him and injuring some of his staff. William Walton Kerr is buried in Boscon Cemetery. He was a native of Cummersdale near Carlisle, where the Border Regiment had its Regimental Depot and HQ, and is commemorated on the war memorial in the churchyard of Our Lady and St Joseph's, Warwick Road, Carlisle. He was educated at St Patrick's RC School, long since demolished and replaced by the Newman RC School, which has a photograph of Lieutenant Colonel Kerr in the entrance hall.

To continue the tour, return to the car and continue along what was Gordon Road. A fork in the road appears after only a couple of hundred metres; the track going off to the left was Connaught Road, and leads to the one-time supply base and railhead at Campiello, on the main road up to the plateau from the plains, and the A31. The erstwhile Connaught Road is very steep, and surfaced with stones and gravel. It should be avoided by car drivers, but can be negotiated on foot or

Boscon War Cemetery, winter 1918/19. Archive OBLI

Boccheta Paù: Gladdens' Rock, British troops admiring the view of the escarpment and the Val d'Astico. Note the zig-zag of the mule track. IWM Q26619

mountain bike.

Continue along Gordon Road, which skirts the western edge of large stony hollow which in 1918 was crowded with the huts and dumps of the Carriola Divisional Headquarters site. In 1944 the hollow was used as a parachute DZ (Dropping Zone) by a Special Operations Executive team. The site is not so far from where Hugh Dalton served

Carriola Base: Field Ambulance Reception Area, October 1918. IWM Q25875

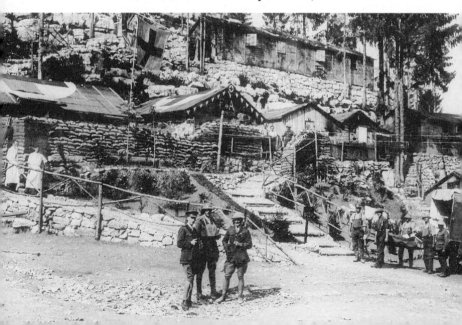

in 1918; in 1940 he was the first Director of the SOE. The road bears right at what was once Sausage Corner (a Kite-Balloon site) and became Cavan Road. The track runs along the northern edge of the hollow, which houses two *malghe*, seasonal mountain dairies, where cheese-making and sometimes butter and sausage production is carried out by families or small co-operatives. Some sell coffee and light snacks in the summer season, a welcome break in a trek or drive through the woods. Cavan Road leads to a junction close to *Malga Carriola*, and from there the tourist can either:

a) return to the fork above Cavaletto, join what was Longdin Crescent for Tattenham Corner, and on to Asiago for the start of the next tour, or

b) turn right down Cavan Road, and follow in the footsteps of 1/8 Worcesters, according to Corbett:

We marched through a great village of hutments, or rather chalet, called Carriola, where Divisional HQ were roughing it ....

On Cavan Road, about 400 metres from the junction, a track on the right leads into **General's Valley**, once the site of the Divisional HQ and Mess. This is where General Fanshawe, GOC 48th Division, fretted during the Austrian onslaught in the morning of 15 June 1918, and where he was visited by General Cavan. The battle was not one controllable by any HQ, as the telephone lines had been cut, and visual contact with brigade and battalion HQs rendered useless by fog and smoke. General Cavan did not interfere in Fanshawe's' attempts to find out what was happening, wisely realising there was nothing to be done at that stage except move reserve battalions up onto the plateau to wherever there was room for them, and keep in contact with the flanking Italian and French HQs. After the battle General Fanshawe was sent home; something for which Cavan was criticized for many years. But a more objective review of events indicates that Cavan acted calmly and intelligently during the battle and at other times in the campaign. His report on Fanshawe must have been fair, as he (Fanshawe) was appointed to another command, admittedly that of a home-based division. At the time of the June battle

Maj Gen Sir Robert Fanshawe, GOC 48th (South Midlands) Division (post-war photograph). Archive OBLI

Carriola: General's Valley; Maj Gen Shoubridge, GOC 7th Division, and staff officers studying a terrain model. IWM Q25881

Fanshawe may have been suffering from 'flu, or its after-effects, and was probably in agonies over the fate of his battalions, batteries and headquarters in the woods along the Ghelpac. He needed a rest, and the British may have needed a scapegoat to placate the Italians. The truth will probably never be known, but Fanshawe was not disgraced, and Cavan seems to have acted with fairness in difficult circumstances.

Continue in Corbett's footsteps down Cavan Road

.... down an endless hill, past a cross-roads called Handley Cross (dear name)

[Corbett is referring to a famous 1890s fox-hunting book: *Handley Cross, or Mr Jorrock's Hunt*, by John Surtees Smith, long out of print but in 2002 could be found in full on the internet at *www.blackmask.com.*]

.... and a beautiful hospital, which has often appeared in illustrated journals, and a sawmill, to the Boscon Sector.

The hospital was probably Swiss Cottage premises occupied by one of the divisional Field Ambulances. There is only a shallow hollow at the side of the road to be found now, on the west side of the road, about 400 metres north of Boscon Cemetery. The sawmill, manned by a couple of RE tradesmen and infantrymen in working parties, was possibly near the disused quarry east of Princes' Road, north of Boscon Cemetery.

Also somewhere along this road was Jerry's Joy, a soup kitchen originally opened to provide mountain rations (soup) for men of supply columns, mule-trains or lorries, moving at night down Prince's Road ruined farm called Ave) wrote:

> *When the month of June began, we were out on patrol between the lines. No Man's Land hereabouts was very hilly, and the night was filled with fantastic shadows, thrown out by the walls of boulders that divided the fields and tracks, or with the occasional gaunt shape of a derelict building, sticking up, white and ghostly, into the twilight. Behind us our own positions were shrouded in the darkness of the massed pines, whose tops only were silhouetted against the starry sky. In front the plateau rolled away in billows that seemed much steeper in the night than they really were. For most of the time everything was quiet - except for the exaggerated clatter of our feet against every loose stone, as we patrolled cautiously between the spurs. Every shadow-making boulder was a promising hiding place for lurking foes - though clearly the Austrians, unlike the Germans, were not habitually in lurking mood. Over towards the enemy positions, well in front of Asiago town, all was still. Yet we knew that the enemy was also on the prowl and holding strong points not far away. Towards the morning our presence was detected and we were subjected to a bombardment of rifle-grenades, which whirled over with a peculiarly hesitating swish and burst spitefully among the rocks. We withdrew at daybreak without a casualty.*

In addition to patrolling and picqueting the central plain, the British and French quickly mounted an aggressive and sustained campaign of trench raiding. First battalion off the mark was 11/Sherwood Foresters, who mounted a fighting patrol at the end of their second day in the trenches in the M. Kaberlaba sector. On the night of 30/31st March a patrol, consisting of two sections from No 11 Platoon, B Company, under Second Lieutenant HL Swire, with Sergeant HW Redfearn as Patrol NCO, conducted a sweep of the ground in front of the line of newly-established and as yet unwired picquet positions. The patrol was to search the tiny hamlet of Coda, suspected of being an enemy outpost. The patrol found no trace of the enemy in or around the buildings, although there were signs of recent occupation. The patrol

Kaberlaba 1998: View N to across the Ghelpac Valley to the northern mountains. FM

then moved north-east along the valley of the river Ghelpac for 750 metres to another hamlet, Moevar. This lay at a crossroads and was only two hundred metres or so from the enemy forward trenches along a railway embankment. One building was found to be occupied by a *k.u.k.* picquet. The Foresters attacked the position and killed all but three of the defenders, without any interference from the garrison of the front line trenches. The survivors, three Hungarians from the 38th Honvéd Division, were taken prisoner; the first, but by no means the last, captives taken from enemy positions on the Asiago Plateau by the British Army.

The patrol members were well rewarded for their efforts. Generals Cavan and Babington (GOC 23rd Division) telegraphed their congratulations, and the GOC 70 Brigade, Brigadier H Gordon, added his personal commendation to all concerned. And there were medals:

> **London Gazette 16 September 1918 T/Second Lieutenant HL Swire:** *Military Cross 'For conspicuous gallantry and devotion to duty. He led his platoon out about 1,000 yards to a group of houses. Disposing his men to cover necessary points, he himself searched the houses with a sergeant and one man,*

Kaberlaba 1993. View North-East across the central plain to Asiago. FM

western end the line ran through thick forest, then across open ground in full view of the enemy. The trenches had been blown out of the underlying rock as there was only a thin covering of soil. Two kilometres behind the front line lay a reserve line, with a second line of resistance about three kilometres further back again.

French-Italian Military Cemetery, Conco, the Concrete Cockerel, 1923

The salient mentioned above encompassed Capitello Pènnar, a low summit at the south-western end of a short ridge. The opposite end of this ridge terminates above a shallow valley; in 1918 it harboured a *k.u.k.* salient built around a redoubt in the village of Bertigo. Capitello had been fortified by the Italians and turned into a strong point. It had to be occupied to deny the enemy observation of the allied line.

The front line, as noted above, looped out and round Capitello

French-Italian Military Cemetery, Conco, 1999. Vittorio Corà

French-Italian Military Cemetery, Conco, 1923.

Pènnar, which takes its name from the eponymous village nearby, but in British War Diaries is usually referred to as Capitello. It provided good observation of some of the *k.u.k.* front and support lines the rear areas of Asiago and of stretches of No Man's Land as far as the Valle Frenzela. In turn Capitello was overlooked by *k.u.k.* defences on M. Sìsemol, another prominent mound some three hundred feet higher than Capitello. Sìsemol was the frequent target for allied Artillery and its approaches were the objective of several large raids. In return *k.u.k.* artillery blasted any movement spotted on Capitello, and pushed saps out from Bertigo towards the French salient, to keep its garrison under close observation.

The French established some picquet outposts in the broken country north of their sector, and conducted random patrols at night to ensure they

were not disturbed, nor their wire interfered with by enemy wire-cutting teams. The French did not spend as much time blowing new trenches as the British; they simply accepted much of what they found, and adapted their defence plans to meet the layout. Also, having only two divisions, there was little manpower to spare for any but essential engineering work, such as strengthening wire aprons and dugouts. General Graziani decided to conform to Italian practice and use linear

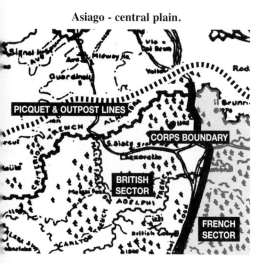

Asiago - central plain.

PICQUET & OUTPOST LINES

CORPS BOUNDARY

BRITISH SECTOR

FRENCH SECTOR

defence (fill the front line with troops) rather than layered (defence in depth, progressively to absorb the force of an assault) to meet any enemy offensive. There was one important exception, which had a key part in defeating the subsequent assault on their sector. In the event of a major attack, Capitello was to be evacuated, and used to trap the attackers within its perimeter.

The French and British named all trenches, enemy and allied, as matter of routine. The

CIMA ECHAR

CAPITELLO PÈNNAR

BERTIGO

ASIAGO

French were allocated the *k.u.k.* trenches south and east of Asiago as far as Bertigo, and gave them names beginning with B, including *Tranchée des Bataille, Bagne, Barbares, Bandits, Balafre,* (which protected Sìsemol) and *Bouc,* leading to Bertigo. The Italians did not generally apply names to trenches; they were referred to by their altitude above sea level in metres, e.g. Quota 1136; Italian officers carried pocket altimeters. It is unclear what was used on the flat ground along the Piave, and in the rear defence lines on the plain around Padua and Vicenza, or on *bunds* in the Venetian lagoons.

The French had a forward HQ and supply base in the *Valle Granezza di Gallio,* a large clearing in a shallow valley, and almost a mirror image of the British base in the adjacent *Valle Granezza di Asiago.* A road ran through the clearing and south to join the Marginal Road near Tattenham Corner. The main Corps HQ, under the control of a General Nourisson, was in a comfortable mansion, the *Villa Carli* outside Marson, a small town on the edge of the Venetian plain, this lay between Marostica and Bassano. It was close to the Sixth Army forward HQ in the *Villa Scaroni,* north of Breganze, and the British GHQ in Lonedo. There were French supply dumps and depots in several towns and villages on the plain, including an artillery HQ in Piovene, controlling heavy and super-heavy (railway) guns and howitzers (see below); and near Vicenza. GQG Forces *Francais en Italie* was housed in the *Villa Camerini,* on M. Berico Vicenza, with

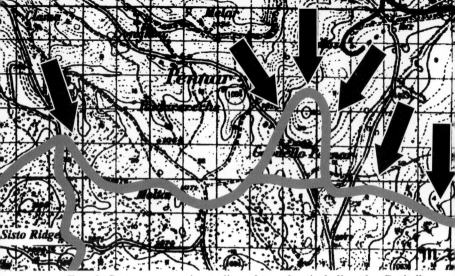

French Sector - approximate line of trenches including the Capitello Pènmar 'Trap'.

offices and minor HQs in the villages of Valmarana and Arcugnano in the nearby *Colli Berici*.

The large concentration of artillery supporting the French Corps along the Piave was split up in early March. Some batteries returned to France, but at least four groups of heavy artillery were redeployed to the escarpment to provide additional fire support for not only XII Corps but also for the remainder of Sixth Army. Two Groups (6 x 155mm guns) were moved into the Brenta valley, one each in Campolongo Sul Brenta and Campese, where they could engage targets on the Asiago Plateau and on Grappa. Another Group of 155mm guns moved onto the plateau and occupied positions along the edge of the escarpment, with batteries in the vicinity of M. Paù and Cima di Fonte, from where they could engage targets in the northern hills and the Val d'Assa. The fourth Group, with 145 mm guns, was located in the foothill villages of Salcedo and Calvene (one source quotes 'Sarcedo', but that is another seven kilometres back from the escarpment, so the alternative quotation of Salcedo is more likely to be correct). The 145s shared the villages with some Italian heavy guns, and British and Italian rear echelons, who did not like having artillery in their midst, especially on 15 June when Austrian long-range guns apparently attempted some counter-battery work and dropped a number of shells among the unsuspecting storemen. Finally, a solitary 381mm railway gun, nicknamed *La Corse*, moved up to sidings west of Thiene, which it shared with Italian weapons of similar type and size. There was close co-operation between the allied artillery arms,

132

achieved through the efforts of the highly-respected Italian General Segre, the senior artillery officer in the Sixth Army. The French and RFC (RAF from 1 April 1918) contingents had an integrated artillery intelligence and control system. The RAF used both aircraft and balloons for fire-control and observation, while Flash Spotters and Sound Rangers of 6 Field Survey Company RE, and No 4 Observation Group, Lovat's Scouts (Sharpshooters), plus divisional, brigade and battalion observers provided additional intelligence for counter-battery missions.

Support Services

The French made considerable use of horses in Italy, more than the British. The standard of horse-care drew some adverse comments from British officers, but vets and farriers noted that the horses may have looked uncurried, but they were fit, strong and well-fed, and treated with rough affection by their handlers. The French used eight horses to draw their carts up the escarpment roads, rather than the British teams of six. British observers noted that the French drivers had all eight horses pulling as one, and that the driver and his mate worked as a team. The French made less use than the British or Italians of lorries and light trucks, but availed themselves of the cableways, and an electric trolley-line, *filovie*, running up a war road from Breganze to Granezza; supplies or passengers for the French sector were off-loaded near Tattenham Corner.

Operation Radetzky

This was the code name given to the western thrust of what turned out to be the last major offensive by the armies of the Austro-Hungarian Empire. A corresponding eastern thrust was named *Operation Albrecht*; a lesser, diversionary, attack in the far west of the Italian-Austrian front line was *Operation Lawine*. (To be precise there was one further offensive by the *k.u.k.*, in southern Serbia during August 1918, but it was in reality a counter-offensive against an Italian advance north of the Albanian port of Valona intended to push the Austrians away from the Otranto Barrage).

Operation Radetzky as it affected the French and especially the British, is described in the various books mentioned earlier, but in essence the *k.u.k.* attempted to breach the Allied lines on the Asiago Plateau and on the Montello. The aim, roughly, was to provoke another Caporetto pursuit, with the hope of knocking Italy out of the war, or at least of reaching a negotiated peace on this front, similar to that achieved on the Eastern Front.

The *k.u.k.* made careful preparations, and in the early hours of 15 June 1918 initiated Radetzky with a very heavy artillery barrage on the Allied front line. That was followed up by infantry attacks spearheaded by storm troops (the *k.u.k.* were early converts - 1916 - to this development) which were closely followed by masses of foot soldiers, machine-gun teams and light artillery detachments. On the plateau the enemy pierced the Allied line in three sectors. Firstly, a deep salient was made in the east, the sector held by XIII (It) Corps with two divisions. The enemy were not expelled for some days, and then with some help from the French (see below). Secondly, a brief breach was made in the front line of the right British division (23rd) at San Sisto Ridge. This was cleared within a few hours, with the help of the flanking French formation (see below). And thirdly, a larger breach was made in the centre of the sector held by the left British division, the 48th (South Midlands). That was not cleared for 24 hours. The French did not yield any ground except by intent, and fought a tenacious battle throughout the 15th June.

Defence of Pènnar and the Barental Road entry.

The 23e Division was in the line, with several battalions of 24e Division in the reserve lines or on stand-by in the foothills. The French had not only read the intelligence reports predicting an enemy offensive, but in early June had mounted a raid on the Bertigo redoubt, which produced prisoners, documents and sight of stock piles of material indicating an attack was imminent. These included field gun ammunition but no guns, drums of telephone cable, and coils of barbed wire.

On 14 June General Graziani returned to his HQ from a meeting with General Montuori, GOC Sixth Army, and discussed the situation with Generals Odry and Bonfant. They recognised that the roads in their tactical area (Barental Road, inclusive to British sector but forming the corps boundary; the road through the *Valle di Granezza di Gallio*) would be enemy objectives as they offered fast, direct access to the plains, and rich pickings in the Valle supply dumps. They reviewed the Sixth Army defence plans, and their own. These included a local counter-preparation barrage for times when an enemy force might be moving towards assembly areas, including the valley behind Pènnar and Bertigo, and reverse slopes beyond a hamlet called Zocchi.

It was also decided to reinforce the front line. Three battalions, one from each of the 24e Division regiments (50, 108,126) were inserted on the left flank, next to 70 Brigade, (British) 23rd Division. This scratch force was commanded by Colonel Bontemps, 126 IR. A battalion of 108 IR was placed next to 11/Sherwood Foresters holding the San Sisto Ridge section as the British battalion was undermanned due to flu, leave, training courses and men employed away from the battalion. The commander of the French company immediately to the right of the Foresters forward company, Lieutenant Gautier, spoke excellent English (he later acted as Liaison Officer with 23rd Division, and for a short time acted as ADC to General Babington when his usual Aide was in hospital). Colonel Bontemps and a Captain Fontan, commanding another company flanking the Foresters, also contacted the British. They probably met the Foresters commanding officer, Lieutenant Colonel Charles Edward Hudson, DSO MC, at Battle HQ behind San Sisto Ridge, and as a result some French personnel (rank and numbers not known) were placed there to ensure that liaison was as good as possible. Owing to a shortage of number, the Foresters could not reciprocate. The French also appear to have liaised with the brigade and divisional HQs to confirm inter-locking arcs of fire for machine-guns covering the road from Asiago.

British support for the French appears to have been limited to a section of 71 Field Ambulance located near Capitello, at a track junction on the rear slopes behind the front line.

Austrian Assault

The Allied counter-preparation artillery barrage commenced at 11.45 pm on 14 June, and continued for some hours, bombarding probable concentration areas, march routes, artillery positions and headquarters. At 3 am the enemy offensive opened with a heavy artillery bombardment and at 3.45 am the French responded with their local counter-preparation barrage, and, according to plan withdrew the defensive screen from Capitello. It was deserted apart from an artillery fire-control team. The salient was heavily bombarded from the front, by guns behind the village of Gallio, and from the vicinity of M. Sisemol. On the flanks it was shelled by guns behind an Austrian redoubt at Sec, forward of San Sisto Ridge, and in Pènnar and Bertigo, up until around 6 am when enemy infantry started moving uphill towards Capitello, and against Italian positions on the right of the French.

Trapped

The enemy assault force consisted of elements from the *k.u.k* 16th

Divison. The leading waves easily breached the wire around Capitello, and 'cleared' the deserted trenches and dug-outs. The enemy then continued down the reverse slope towards the front line, and ran straight into the trap laid by the French. The enemy were engaged at short range by intense small-arms, machine-gun and mortar fire. There was no escape; they were trapped inside the salient, and died like flies. Their colleagues behind tried to help, but there was little they could do. They did not lack courage, and during the course of the morning mounted five attacks against the French line one each side of the salient. Few, if any, enemy troops reached the front line wire, and none were reported to have crossed it. The slaughter was enormous, as it was also among the follow-up waves caught by the Allied artillery on the open slopes of Capitello Ridge around Bertigo, and on the forward slope of M. Sìsemol. No records of the *k.u.k.* by sector have been located, but one estimate put the losses in dead and severely injured around the salient as not less than 2,000.

There was one more large attack, by troops who had been assembled in the dead ground north of Pènnar, but this too was defeated, as were two attempts to attack along the line of the road from Asiago, by infantry emerging from the Sec redoubt. These two attacks were broken up by French and British machine-gun and artillery fire.

Little information has been located about the assistance given to the XIII (It) Corps manning the sector on the right flank of the French. The Italian Corps had only two divisions, 14° and 24°, and both were on the plateau, manning trenches running across open slopes for about 5,500 metres. A prominent feature to the rear of the line, M. Ekar, had been turned into a redoubt, and was also garrisoned by the Corps. Immediately to the right of the inter-corps boundary the line swung sharply to the rear, towards the foot of M. Ekar, then turned north again to another mound, M. Val Bella. Beyond that the line, occupied by the XX Corps, ran along more slopes and down into, and across, the Val Brenta, and up onto the eastern flank of Grappa.

The enemy assault was made by troops from three *k.u.k.* divisions: *42nd Honvéd, 26th Schutzen* and the *Edelweiss Corps* (a division-sized formation), the last two composed of mountain troops who fought an almost personal war against the Italians, especially *Alpini* regiments.

The enemy penetrated the Italian line and created a salient about two miles wide and up to three miles deep.

The French 'presented a defensive flank', to use the old phrase, to the breach and for fifteen days held it against infiltration, attack and artillery bombardment, while harassing the enemy within the salient by all means possible. The Italians mounted several counter-attacks, and cleared some of the ground. Finally, on 29-30 June, again with help from the French (mainly artillery and machine-gun barrages), they cleared the salient of enemy and restored the line.

On 16 June French patrols probed forward to locate the enemy. They, however, had retired from the scene to their support lines, but the patrols captured a few prisoners, including some from the vicinity of Pènnar.

The infantry regiments involved in the June 1918 battle were awarded a Battle Honour: *Offensive autrichienne du 15 juin sur le front italien.* Officers, and possibly Warrant Officers, present on the plateau during the fighting were awarded an Italian commemorative medal, struck on the authority of GOC Sixth Army, General Luca Montuori, to commemorate the defence of the *Altipiano* during the offensive.

TOUR J

The French Forces on the Plateau

Start: Asiago station car park.
Maps: Altipiano di Asiago Tourist Board Great War map; *Foglio Sud* [South Sheet]
Itinerary: Drive out of the car park away from the Ice Stadium, turn *right* at the main road, drive into the centre of Asiago to a T-junction. Turn *left*, drive to *Gallio*, turn *right* in the centre of the town, then left for *Sìsemol*.

Drive up to the village, park and walk round the hill by a footpath on the right (west) side and study the ground towards Bertigo and Pènnar. The Capitello is a surprisingly innocuous-looking flat mound. Even a brief stop reveals the tactical value of both M. Sìsemol and. the Capitello. (Both Gallio and Sìsemol are worth visiting in their own right.)

Return to the main road from Gallio, turn *left*, then *left* at the T-junction. Bertigo is on the left at the next junction, but in 2001 it did not appear to have any relics of the Great War, so continue on up the road. Capitello Pènnar is the summit on the far end of the ridge on the right of the road. The summit can be reached by parking on the short road which appears to the right, or thereabouts, and a rough scramble to the top. It provided a good OP, but a poor position to hold in the face of a determined attack, and a superb target for artillery in the northern hills.

The trenches held by the French can be found in the undergrowth on either side of the road from Gallio, beyond the Camping Ekar site, and they can be followed for some distance in either direction. To the west they lead to the trenches manned by British between March and November 1918; the front line trench (Alhambra Trench) and the reserve one (Adelphi Trench) at San Sisto Ridge see below.

To the east the remnants of the front line can be traced for at least 1kilometre from the Gallio road, and into the Italian-held sector.

Return to the car, and continue along the road from Gallio. At the main road (Asiago - Bassano del Grappa) there is a memorial commemorating the role of the people of the Altopiano killed in the struggle for peace; it is at a location marked Turcio on maps. At one time it was possible to drive along a forest track running the length of the *Valle di Granezza di Gallio*, but in recent years it has been signed as closed to motor traffic, and in any case was, at least in the late 1990s, not the best road in Italy. It is possible to drive along a forest track running down through the Val Campo Rossignolo, in 1918 a French support area, to the Marginal Road and Tattenham Corner. However, check with the Asiago tourist office as forest roads can be signed as 'closed' any time to keep motor traffic, cyclists and pedestrians away from logging operations.

Adelphi Trench - the French Connection

At the junction with the main Asiago-Bassano del Grappa road, turn **right** and drive for 1km and then **left** at the junction into the forest. After about 600 metres turn left - there should be two CWGC signs pointing right, for Barental and Granezza cemeteries, turn right - and drive up what in 1918 was Barental Road. After about 500 metres, (not 150, as stated in *Asiago*!) look for a concrete barbecue stand on the right. Park next to it, and walk amongst the rocks on the Asiago side (the way you came in) of the stand and the eastern end of Adelphi Trench appears. It can be followed to the east, away from the barbecue stand, as far as the track from Turcio, and into the forest beyond for at least 500 metres. This was the reserve trench for the French left flank, probably used to feed reinforcements into the 11/Sherwood Foresters lines during the Austrian incursion of 15 June 1918.

Alhambra Trench

The remains of Alhambra Trench can be found at the foot of the northern slope of San Sisto Ridge. Drive back down Barental road, turn left and then right and park close to where the forest track joins the Asiago-Bassano road. As of 2001 there was only a suggestion of a track, so walk up into the woods parallel to, and about 25 metres away from, the verge (to keep clear of rock faces) and after about 150 metres the remains of the trench can be found (with difficulty) in the undergrowth.

The trench, or parts of it, can also be found on the far side of the main road, and followed for at least a kilometre through the forest, but it is more a maze than a line of trenches and sprigs, and it is very difficult to make any sense of the layout. This section of the line, the French name for the trench has not so far been located, can also be reached from a small camping-cum-leisure area. It is at the end of a short track, the first turning on the right towards Asiago from the Barental Road/main road junction. [The author has not explored that route, and is indebted to John Chester, of the Spalding and South Lincolnshire Branch of the Western Front Association, a veteran explorer of the Asiago battleground and an authority on the Italian campaign, for this information.]

Return to the car. The next tour commences from the junction of the forest track and the main road.

As noted above, the French forces in this section of the front line co-operated with the British on San Sisto Ridge in defeating two attacks mounted by *k.u.k.* infantry along the main road from the direction of Asiago, and appear to have concentrated machine-guns on the slopes to the east of the camping site, covering the line of the road where it climbs up through a shallow re-entrant, and beyond that to what is now the start of the access road for the local hospital, built on the site of a pre-1914 holiday home, the *Villa Dal Brun*. Beyond the hospital is a large farm, Sec, in 1918 the closest permanently manned *k.u.k.* position to the British, if not the Allied, front line on the plateau. It was from the rear of the Sec redoubt that the troops for the two enemy attacks mentioned above emerged onto the ground either side of the main road, around 9.30 am on 15 June. French and British artillery and machine-gun fire shattered both attempts to advance down the road, and thereafter the Allied forces in this section of the front were left in peace by the *k.u.k.* infantry, but not their artillery, which remained active more or less up to the day before the Armistice. The Allied infantry, however, did not allow the Austrians any peace, especially any unlucky enough to be sent to garrison the Sec redoubt. It was heavily raided right up until the start of the final Allied advance, on November 1918 across the plateau and through or over the northern mountains into the Austro-Hungarian Empire. The story of one of the last raids on Sec is told below.

Tour K
Sec Redoubt

Introduction

The first British trench raid on the Asiago Plateau took place on the night of 7/8 April, and the last during the night of 29/30 October 1918. The French also initiated trench raids in April, and mounted their last on the night of 31 October/1 November. The Italians had conducted raids against *k.u.k.* trenches from May 1915 until the end of October 1918, and the enemy had responded in kind, but with diminishing enthusiasm as the war ground on. The last raid so far identified took place against the British in the Granezza sector on August, 1918.

Between those dates raiding of the enemy lines by the Allied forces was almost continuous, and caused the *k.u.k.* severe problems of wastage of men and material and declining morale. The scale and pattern of the Allied raids gradually increased, culminating in a British 'Grand Slam' on 8/9 August. Five brigades (20, 22, 91, 143, 144) deployed troops from twenty-two companies drawn from eight battalions to mount eight simultaneous raids across the entire *k.u.k.* front line opposite the British Corps sector, from Ambrosini in the west to Ave in the east; the Sec redoubt was raided the next night, in concert with a battalion-sized French raid on M. Sisemol. Teams of Scouts from the battalions holding the front line marked the routes to the objectives and cut gaps in the enemy wire. Much of the rest was destroyed by the main barrage, provided by British, Italian and French batteries. In the Carriola (left) sector two Italian searchlights, one on M. Zovetto, and the other on M. Kaberlaba, provided artificial moonlight, and a bonfire was lit on M. Lemerle as the signal to withdraw. It also acted as a useful marker for raiding parties returning through mist and drifting smoke. The raids were successful; the *k.u.k.* probably lost around 600 dead, wounded and missing, in addition to the 355 prisoners noted on the accompanying map.

The following night the French raid on M. Sisemol was also successful, capturing 241 prisoners; and probably inflicting further losses of 4-500 dead, wounded and missing.

The following description could apply to the methods used by nearly every Allied raid on the plateau.

Sec Redoubt

On the night of 10 September, as part of an inter-Allied programme of raids, the British raided a *k.u.k.* stronghold south of Asiago. The objective was Sec (Sech on some maps), in pre-war days a large dairy farm which by 1918 the Austrians had turned into a small fortress, which Allied artillery had turned into a wilderness of craters and ruins. Sec Farm, and the nearby *Villa Dal Brun*, in happier times the holiday-home of an industrialist from Schio, had been used since 1916 by the *k.u.k.* as OPs and patrol bases. Both locations were in a salient reaching out towards the Allied line at San Sisto Ridge. The area north-east of Sec, on ground on either side of a sunken lane, had been used as an assembly area by assault troops on 14 June; and gaps in the wire in front of the farm had been cut by *k.u.k.* sappers who also marked-out forming-up lines just outside the wire, all without attracting the attention of British outposts. Sec was well known to the British and for months it had been raided with almost monotonous regularity. The *k.u.k.* command never took the hint, and replaced one garrison after the previous one had been eliminated. In September Sec was attacked for the last time.

In September the 48th (South Midland) Division was in the Granezza sector with 145 (South Midland) Brigade in the right forward sub-sector, with two battalions in the line, one in support close behind, and the fourth in reserve at Pria dell'Acqua, about two kilometres to the rear. The battalion in support found the troops for raiding parties; in this case the task fell to 1/4 Oxf & Bucks LI. The battalion was at

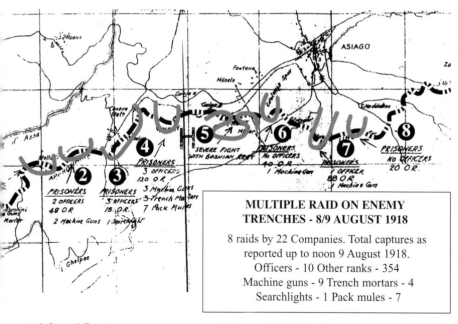

MULTIPLE RAID ON ENEMY TRENCHES - 8/9 AUGUST 1918

8 raids by 22 Companies. Total captures as reported up to noon 9 August 1918.
Officers - 10 Other ranks - 354
Machine guns - 9 Trench mortars - 4
Searchlights - 1 Pack mules - 7

1. 2 Coys 2/Border
2. 2 Coys 20/Manchesters
3. 4 Coys 1/5 Staffs.

4. 2 Coys 1/ R.Welsh F.
5. 3 Coys 1/6 Gloucs
6. 3 Coys 1/8 Worcestershire

that time in the upper end of Adelphi Trench, and in dug-outs and huts in Ilkley Redoubt, near the upper end of Malga Fassa, a large clearing in the forest covering Prinele Ridge, to the south of, and above, San Sisto valley.

The 4th Battalion Oxfordshire and Buckinghamshire Light Infantry was formed in 1908 as part of the Territorial Force. The Battalion headquarters were in Oxford, and there were outlying companies or detachments in surrounding towns such as Banbury, Chipping Norton, Culham, Henley-on-Thames and Witney. It was mobilized in 1914, and crossed to France in March 1915 as part of the South Midland (later 145) Brigade. Despite the carnage of the Western Front the Battalion retained its local character for a long time. A group photograph taken in April 1918 at GHQ Central Schools, Torreglia, shows 165 officers and men who were serving with the unit when it sailed for France: ten of those shown were killed in Italy nine of these during the fighting around Hill 1021 on 15/16 June.

On 6 September the Adjutant, Captain WH Enoch, received a signal from Brigade HQ containing a Warning Order indicating that the Battalion would take part in an attack on Sec at a time and date to be specified. That was followed on 8 September by the Operational Order, which stated that the Battalion, less one platoon, would raid enemy positions on 'X' Day at a time to be notified later. The objectives were:

1. 350 yard stretch of the front line, (*Tranchée de la Bataille* on British maps, but that name does not appear in the various orders, the War Diary or after action report.)
2. dug-outs lining a sunken road to the rear of the front line
3. dug-outs in the front line
4. dug-outs in a communications trench in the rear of the position.

The orders were simple but comprehensive; after five months of raiding, plans were based on well-tested drills, and orders matter of routine. They included artillery support (a protective barrage from Zero hour to Zero + 40 minutes), signals for calling an emergency barrage (a Red Ground Flare), mortar and machine-gun support, the recall signal (Smoke, i.e. Phosphorous, Rifle Grenades fired from a 'cup discharger', and resembling a *Golden Rain* firework), prisoner handling, the location of a Checking-In Post, and of a Brigade Forward Report Centre (BFRC) in No Man's Land.

The BFRC was not involved with the execution of the raid. The small team of officers and men manning the centre had three tasks: first, to establish and maintain contact with higher headquarters during the raid. Second, to evaluate and report any enemy response such as a counter-attack on the raiding force or an assault on the front line which would require action initiated and controlled by Brigade, Division or Corps HQs , and, third, to provide a replacement command team if the raid ran into serious opposition and the officers were killed. Siting the BFRC in No Man's Land was a sensible precaution, and demonstrates the extent to the British Army had developed its command and control procedures by late 1918.

Preparation

The Commanding Officer, Lieutenant Colonel AJN Bartlett DSO, was on leave, so the Second-in-Command, Major Percy Pickford DSO MC, was responsible for planning and mounting the raid. He worked closely with the Adjutant, Captain W H Enoch, and the Battalion Intelligence Officer, Second Lieutenant JT Foster. That officer arranged for the battalion Scouts, who were under his command, to make an earth model of the objective and the surrounding terrain in the Malga Fassa area to help Major Pickford plan the raid and draft the orders. The model was also used on 7 September when he briefed the four company commanders (and representatives from the artillery, mortar and machine-gun units supporting the raid). After the briefing Major Pickford, the Adjutant and the company commanders went to an OP on *Cima del Taglio*, in the French sector (described in some detail by Hugh Dalton) to study the ground and the routes to and from the objective. Later, after evening Stand-To, the company commanders and an escort moved out into No Man's Land to reconnoitre the Forming-Up position at Midway House, some 800 metres from the front line lines. They were accompanied part of the way by the Battalion Medical Officer who would have wanted to check on his temporary Dressing Station for the raid, a dug-out forward of the front line (Alhambra Trench), at the side of a track running from San Sisto Ridge down through a small glen and out across No Man's Land to Asiago.

The following day, Sunday 8th, around the model, the company commanders in turn briefed their platoon commanders, who then briefed the men. Battalion orders were issued on 9 September and dealt with such matters as routes out and in, dress (officers to wear camouflage, i.e. soldiers jacket, trousers and puttees, and carry rifles; no sticks to be carried), identification - white bands on each upper arm, different widths for each assault group - and that artificial moonlight would be provided by a searchlight on M. Kaberlaba. In addition, as part of a wider deception plan, Major Pickford had arranged for a dummy raid on Sec at 11.30 pm 9 September, and for another to be made 'at another place' (on the *k.u.k.* redoubt at Ave) at Zero Hour - 4 am, 10 September.

At 10.28 pm OC D Company, Captain JE Boyle, and twelve men moved out to lay white webbing tapes marking the forming up line. (D Company provided two platoons as left and right flank guards for the raiding force; the rest remained in the support lines as guards and duty-men, under the Regimental Sergeant Major).

The Battalion Scouts and two Lewis Gun Sections from D Company, all under Second Lieutenant Foster, moved out at 00.55 am to secure the Forming-Up Line (FUL).

Captain and Adjutant WH Enoch, awarded an MC for his role in the attack of 10 September 1918 Archive OBLI

At 1.30 am the Battalion HQ party, Commanding Officer, Adjutant, Medical Officer and stretcher bearers (the Drum and Bugle Corps) and the Padre, Captain The Reverend Henderson CF, moved off. The MO, stretcher-bearers and the padre moved into the dug-out in Alhambra Trench, while the rest of the HQ party continued on to the FUL.

By 2.00 am the Scouts, flank guards and taping party were in position by Midway House and Captain Boyle had commenced marking the route to the FUL, and the line itself.

At 3.45 am the raiding parties were in position along the FUL.

Major Percy Pickford DSO MC, (right) Acting CO at the time of the raid on Sec. Archive OBLI

At 4.00 am the barrage opened, and the raiders moved off towards their objectives, lead by a wire-cutting party from A Company equipped with long-handled wire cutters and cutting gloves. The raiders moved quickly up to, and through the wire, and attacked their objectives. In the words of the Battle Narrative written by Major Pickford and Captain Enoch:

> *Barrage The barrage throughout was perfect, the 18pdr shell with 106 fuse being very effective and no shorts reported although the leading men kept within 50 yards of it. Two or three casualties were reported from the SUNKEN LANE, this was probably due to our men encountering less resistance than was expected and getting ahead*

144

of the Time Table. The smoke shell on AVE was useful and the enemy was entirely deceived as to where the attack was taking place. The 6" Newton Mortars put up a good show on the Front Line Branch running NE.

And:

Right Platoon *A Coy A machine gun was seen in the NEWTON barrage east of the SUNKEN rd firing towards MIDWAY HOUSE. This was engaged until plus 15 by L.G, and then rushed simultaneously by the L.G. section and Bombing Section. The gun was captured also one prisoner ....*

Centre Platoon A Coy *Section spread left and right* [along the line of the main trench] *... the dug-out in the Communication* [trench] *was then dealt with by smoke grenade thrown in and four of the enemy emerged on fire; they were put out of their misery with the bayonet.*

Left Platoon A Coy *Left section told to work up to dugout 50 yds W. of road found 6 enemy dead in Front Line (confirmed by C Coy Platoon going through later) & captured two alive. The dugout could not be recognised. L.G. Section got five prisoners at LONE TREE HOUSE.*

Most of the trenches and dugouts had suffered severely from the barrage, and many of the enemy had been killed, severely wounded or had voted with their feet and disappeared to the rear.

Aftermath

By 6.30 am the raiding party had reported back to Malga Fassa, where, according to the Battalion War Diary, *breakfast was served after which the men turned in for well-earned rest.*

The raid netted thirty-seven prisoners, including one officer and three machine-guns, and claimed to have killed a large number of enemy. The Battalion suffered one man killed in action, two missing and eight wounded, including the Padre. The Reverend Henderson was seriously injured when the RAP was hit by a 4.2 inch shell during a retaliatory *k.u.k.* barrage, but survived. Of the other wounded three died, one in the RAP and the others in the AOS, Cavaletto. The dead were Corporal William John Rollings, B Company, who was moved to the AOS by ambulance from the RAP and lingered for two weeks before dying on 23 September. He was the son of John and Ellen Rollings, of Rotherfield Peppard, a small village near Henley-on-Thames. Also moved direct to Cavaletto from the RAP was Lance Corporal Ernest Frank Taylor, age 21, son of Alfred and Laura Taylor, of Bletchington, Oxford, who died later that day; both are buried in Cavaletto Cemetery. Private Frank Kingdom, a Devon man, age 25, son of Richard Kingdom, Witheridge, North Devon, died in the RAP shortly after being brought in by the stretcher bearers. Private Frederick William Nash, age 20 and the son of Thomas Busby and Sophia Nash, 26, Leopold Street, North Oxford, was killed during the raid. Both men were probably buried in the northern-most Barental Road war cemetery (there were two, the other was close to the Pria dell'Acqua road junction), and moved to the Granezza Cemetery when the war cemeteries were cleared by the Imperial War Graves Commission in 1919-1920.

Awards

The battalion received congratulations from General Cavan, General Sir HB Walker (GOC 48th Division), Brigadier WW Pitt-Taylor (GOC 145 Brigade), and Major A Russell, commanding 240th Brigade, RFA. Captain JE Boyle, OC D Company, was awarded a Military Cross, the citation reading:

For conspicuous gallantry and devotion to duty during a raid. Under considerable enemy shelling he sited and taped out a forming-up line out of enemy observation, and from this he ran forward tapes for each leading platoon. He then personally placed the party in the line and pointed out to platoon commanders their exact objectives. During the raid, despite an enemy barrage, he laid out tapes towards the enemy's front line to guide the raiding party back, and he did not return to our lines until the whole party was in.

(As a point of interest, at the time of the raid Captain Boyle was a substantive Second Lieutenant, Acting Captain. James Eyre Boyle was a native of Bootle, Liverpool and before the Great War had served in the 3rd Volunteer Battalion Cheshire Regiment (Cyclist Corps). He enlisted into 5/Cheshire on 8 September 1914, giving his age as 27 years. By April 16 he had been promoted to Company Sergeant Major and had been Mentioned In Dispatches for *"gallant and distinguished conduct in the field"*. A year later he was a Second Lieutenant in 1/4 Oxf & Buck. He survived the war and returned to civilian life on 19 March 1919, finding work as an agent for the Provincial Insurance Co. in Crewe, Cheshire).

There were also awards of the Military Cross to Captain Enoch, Second Lieutenants WRB Brooks and JF Wright. The citation for Wilfred Brooks read in part;

146

> *During a raid on 10/9/18 this officer was the first to enter the enemy trench. He found a post at the point of entry and immediately charged it, capturing an officer and four men. He then organised his platoon so as to cover the left flank of the attack, and remained in the enemy lines until the whole raiding party was out. He displayed fine dash and good leadership.*

There was an award of a Distinguished Conduct Medal to 200410 Cpl. FR Crumbleholme. He was commanding a section in one of the flank guards when an enemy machine-gun team moved into position to his front and opened fire. To quote from the citation for his award:

> *...he immediately took his section and rushed the gun. After a hand-to-hand fight in which the officer attempted to bayonet him he succeeded in killing the officer and capturing the gun and the remainder of the team.*

In addition, there were awards of thirteen Military Medals, and two Bars to Military Medals.

In addition to the British decorations, slightly later there were seven

A Company 1/4 Oxf & Bucks LI officers, Spring 1918 Captain JE Boyle (seated right); 2/Lt WRB Brooks standing, centre. (One subaltern 1/1 Bucks Bn Oxf & Bucks LI standing left.) Archive OBLI

awards of Italian medals, including a *Medaglia d' Argento Al Valor Militare* to Major Pickford and Captain WP Powell, commanding C Company. The citation for Major Pickford noted that:

> *As Battalion Commander he gave proof of great courage in carrying out an attack on 1/0/9/18 against strongly fortified enemy positions south of Asiago, attack which had been accurately prepared by him. By his personal example he inspired his command to the brilliant attainment of all their allotted tasks.*

Captain Powell's citation recorded that:

> *.... he lead his company in the attack on 10/9/18 and carried out the difficult operation of attacking the enemy front line from behind with great success. Although burned by a smoke grenade which exploded prematurely, he continued to direct the attack and set an example to all ranks.*

Three members of the battalion were doubly rewarded for their efforts. Second Lieutenant JF Wright MC and Corporal Crumbleholme DCM were each a *Medaglia della Bronzo Al Valor Militare*. Three Corporals were awarded the *Croce di Guerra*, for bravery, determination and leadership inside the enemy position and one, Corporal E Rixon MM, B Company, earned his British medal in the raid.

The Italian awards were presented by King Victor Emanuel III at a Royal Review held at Nove, near Marostica on the Venetian plain, on 29 September.

The Raid

Start: end of previous tour: junction of the Asiago-Bassano road, and the one-time Barental Road.

Maps: Altipiano di Asiago Tourist Board Great War map [South Sheet]

Itinerary: From the main road, drive up the forest track, and turn right into another, but rougher, track and through the woods, then past a long, narrow pasture at the bottom of San Sisto ridge, to San Sisto Chapel. Park the car, and walk on along the track to a Y-junction.

Digression: This area is little changed since 1918, and the path to the left runs up-hill to the Malga Fassa clearing which in the 1990s was a dairy pasture; signs politely directed walkers away from the ground. The location of Ilkley Redoubt can be found by following Adelphi Trench from either the one time Barental Road, or the east end of the San Sisto clearing, up through the woods to the top of the ridge. It is not always an easy walk, and there is little left of the redoubt apart from what appear to be filled-in trenches and the remains of dug-outs. A path runs north, left when approaching up Alhambra Trench, and downhill, and skirts the Malga Fassa clearing to reach the Y-junction. (Alhambra Trench continues over the ridge, so keep the northern mountains in view; it is very easy to become disoriented in the forest to the south of Asiago.) The path follows the line of the Star Track of 1918, and was the route taken by the raiding party and the support teams (medical, scouts, signallers, BFRC team) in the early hours of 10 September 1918.

Itinerary (cont): At the Y junction, turn right and walk downhill; this also follows the route taken by the raiding party. Pause at the edge of the forest; Alhambra Trench crossed (or went under) the road at this point, or very close to it, and the remains can be found and followed for some distance in either direction. Various plans for an Allied offensive across the central plain were mooted between March and October 1918; all required artillery and ammunition to be moved forward of the front line to support the leading elements. Where trenches met roads leading to Asiago, Gallio, etc they went across the roads, and the gaps were either bridged with improvised assault bridges, or covered with tree trunks and made into covered trenches.

The trench has been progressively filled-in over the years to make logging operations less dangerous, but can still be found, with some effort. Facing the forest, the right-hand section of the trench can be located about fifty metres into the undergrowth, at your one o'clock. The section on the left, seems to have disappeared, but the rest can be found by walking along a small track at the edge of the trees for about 100 metres, and walking up into the trees; it can be followed to the Asiago-Bassano road, to the point described in the previous tour.

Still standing on the track at the edge of the forest, look to your two o'clock. The corrugated iron roof of Sec farmhouse can be seen amongst some trees to the left of the prominent buildings of the hospital. (Can *usually* be seen; thick mist appears at the most inconvenient times on the plateau.)

The front line barbed wire-apron followed the line of the forest, part inside the tree-line, part outside. The gap by which the raiders passed through the wire was probably on the track, between the edge of the forest and the track Y-junction.

The route of the raiding party can be followed across the pastures; the farmers have in previous years been very tolerant. Otherwise take the right hand lane, which was, at least up to late 2001, very rough

View across the pastures towards the objective, 1999. FM

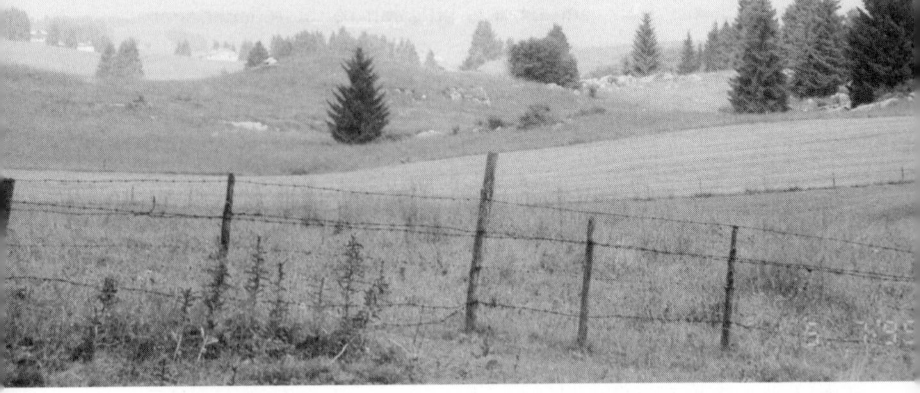

indeed, and only suitable for a four-wheel drive vehicle, hence the walking!

Follow the track for about 600 metres to a road leading left to a cluster of buildings, Guardinalti, on 10 September 1918 the location of the Brigade Forward Report Centre. Further on along the track from San Sisto Ridge, the first house on the left was known to the British as Ave South. In 1918 it was a ruined house used by both sides as a listening post and OP. The British regarded it as their property, but it belonged to whoever got there first. For example, the Ox & Bucks War Diary notes that on 5 September:

a patrol of 12 ORs under Lt. A.L. DAVIS left our lines at 8

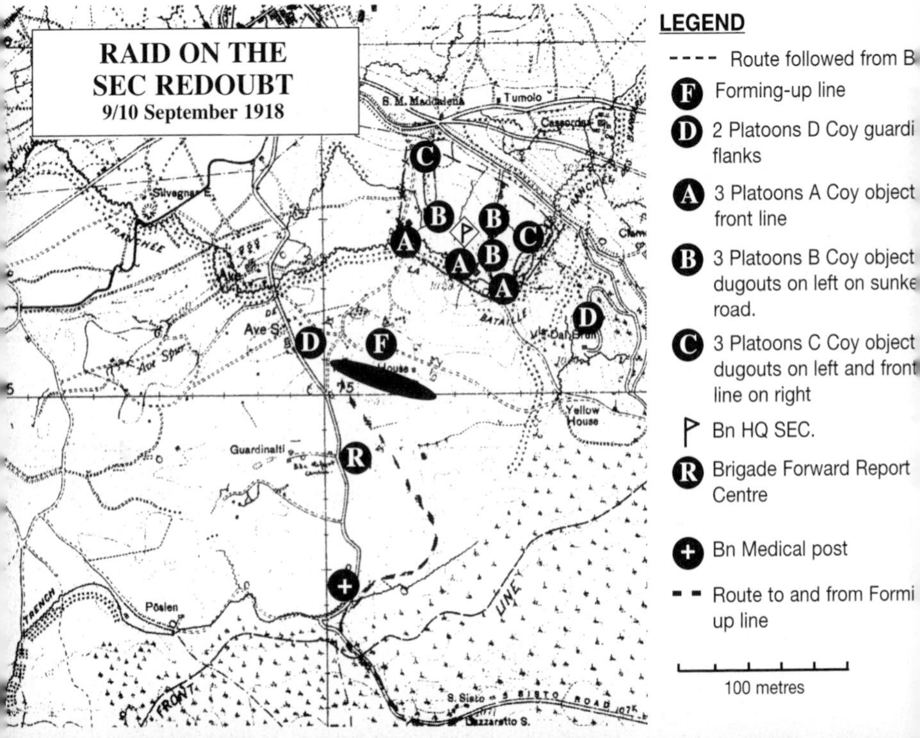
RAID ON THE
SEC REDOUBT
9/10 September 1918
S. M. Maddalena
Tumolo
Silvegna E.
TRANCHEE
Ave S.
Ave Spur
BATAILLE
Yellow House
Guardinalti
Pöslen
TRENCH
FRONT
LINE
S. Sisto
S. SISTO ROAD
Lazzaretto S.
LEGEND
Route followed from B
Forming-up line
2 Platoons D Coy guardi
flanks
3 Platoons A Coy object
front line
3 Platoons B Coy object
dugouts on left on sunke
road.
3 Platoons C Coy object
dugouts on left and front
line on right
Bn HQ SEC.
Brigade Forward Report
Centre
Bn Medical post
Route to and from Formi
up line
100 metres

p.m. to occupy S. Ave. The ruins were occupied by our patrol for one hour and then a strong hostile party estimated at 25-30 strong approached from [a] North Easterly direction. Following a pre-arranged signal our artillery put down a pre-arranged crash and the patrol moved out again, but found the enemy on both sides of S. Ave. Not being strong enough to tackle the enemy returned to our lines 12.30 a.m.

The position of left flank guard is shown on the operational map as being to the east of the house. The guard was probably deployed around the ruins in all-round defence, with the Lewis guns positioned to fire down the line of track from Ave, a k.u.k. redoubt, and half-right over the re-entrant between Ave South and Ave Spur.

The site of the FUL can be found by walking towards Ave, visible ahead left, and turning down the track running away right-rear just before the Ave farm complex. The FUL was in dead ground (to Sec) some 450 metres down this track, about 25 metres off to the right (south) of it, over a slight rise. From there the route can be followed across the fields to the farm, but if there are cows in the pastures it might be better to stay on the track, and walk up to where it joins another one, and turn left. The right flank guard was spread round the ruins of the *Villa Dal Brun*, with the Lewis guns covering the east side of the enemy trench to catch a counter-attack in the flank, and the approaches from enemy outposts in the Clama valley (see air-oblique panaroma, below).

The *Villa Dal Brun* has long since been absorbed into a hospital,

Air-oblique photograph of the objective Archive OBLI

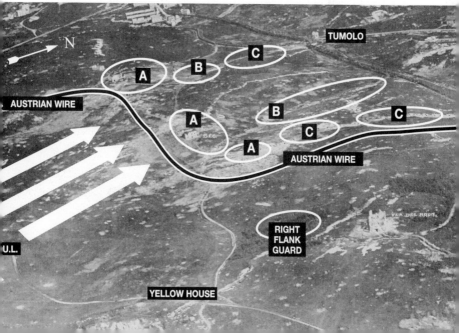

The farmhouse, 2001. Richard Jeffs collection

and as with any care establishment the occupants should be left in peace. Proceed down the track leading to Sec. Once in the vicinity of the farm, a word with the farmer does not go amiss. The enemy trenches ran close to the farmhouse, but disappeared long ago.

The sunken lane can easily be found, and followed downhill to the main road. There is nothing to see of the dug-outs and trenches bombed by the raiders, who had to penetrate a long way, 800 metres, behind the enemy front line, and exposed to machine-gun fire from his support trenches. There were reportedly garrisons in buildings at SM Maddalena and Tumolo, but they do not appear to have interfered with the raiding party.

At the bottom of Sunken Lane there is a good view over a small shallow valley, an area marked Cassoradar on maps old and new. This was the assembly area, and, further right (south) the enemy FUL for the two ill-starred final attacks by *k.u.k.* forces on the Anglo-French corps boundary on 15 June 1918.

The FUL and the objective can also be reached by car. From the San Sisto chapel return to the Asiago-Bassano road, turn left and drive for

The sunken lane 2001. Richard Jeffs collection

N

The Scuola Ski Asiago; houses beyond are SM Maddalena (L) and Tumolo (R) Richard Jeffs collection

about 1.5 kilometres to the sunken lane; look for a *Scuola Ski-Asiago* sign, hut and chair-lift at the bottom of the track. Park and explore.

Redeployment

In mid-October HQ XIV Corps, 7th and 23rd Divisions and most of the supporting arms and services on the plateau were re-deployed from the Asiago Plateau to the Treviso area in readiness for what was to become known as the Battle of Vittorio Veneto. The 48th Divison and truncated supply and service elements remained on the plateau, in the Granezza sector; one French division also remained. The Carriola sector was occupied by elements of the flanking formation, the First (Italian) Army, and the boundary with the Sixth (It) Army was moved east to (roughly) the line M. Sunio-Queen's Corner-Ghelpac Fork. The 48th Division, for tactical purposes only, remained under command of Sixth Army, in XII (It) Corps; the French 24th Division formed part of XX (It) Corps.

The two Allied divisions had one more contribution to make in Italy, when on 1 November they started to advance across the central plain towards the northern mountains. By 3pm 4 November, when the Armistice on this front came into force, leading elements of 48th Division were deep inside Austro-Hungarian territory, in small villages on the far side of the Val Sugana, well beyond the northern rim of the Asiago Plateau. That advance is barely mentioned in the few books available about the British in Italy during the Great War, and merits greater study. (The best description is in *By God, They Can Fight*; see bibliography.) There was little fighting and few casualties but some prodigious feats of climbing and marching.

TOUR L
Dueveille & Montecchio Precalino CWGC Cemeteries

Start: Asiago or the A4/A31 junction.
Maps: LAC Vicenza.
Itinerary: Drive to/along the A31 to the exit for *Dueville*, leave the autostrada and follow the road-signs for Dueville, and drive to the main square, the *Piazza Monza*, by the railway station. Facing the square and the railway station, turn right into the *Via IV Novembre* and at the traffic lights turn left, and into the car park about 200 metres on the right, outside the (new) community cemetery; the CWGC Cemetery is opposite, next to the original town cemetery.

Dueville CWGC Cemetery
When the British corps was deployed onto the Asiago Plateau in March 1918 GHQ BEF(I) established a Casualty Clearing Station in Dueville. The role of the CCS was to care for men seriously injured in the fighting on the plateau or in accidents, in rear areas or at the GHQ Schools. A cemetery was required, and the Italian authorities made ground available next to the town burial ground, close to the CCS which was housed in the village school. Dueville is on the railway line from Vicenza to Thiene, and in 1918 the school was close to the station, making transfer of patients to hospital trains a simple matter. (There were one Italian and four British hospital trains available to the BEF(I) at one time or another, and several large hospitals and convalescent camps near Genoa, and on the Riviera, for the use of the force, and for the seriously injured and sick of the Otranto Barrage.) A branch of the Decauville light railway mentioned earlier ran south from near Breganze, past Montecchio Precalcino to terminate at Dueville station, and it appears to have been used to take not only supplies but sick or injured soldiers to the CCSs in Dueville and Montecchio Precalcino. (There were numerous accidents in the maintenance and supply sites in the foothills, as well as road traffic accidents on the mountain roads.)

The Cemetery Register records 128 British burials. The earliest was that of Gunner Arthur Edmondson of C Battery, 102nd Brigade, Royal Field Artillery, died of wounds on 3 April 1918, age 35 years and the son of John Richard and Elizabeth Edmondson, of Leeds. The last burial was that of William Herron, who died of disease on 28 October 1919. William was 25 years old, and the son of William and Isabel Herron, of 60, Dorset Street, Glasgow. At the time of his death he was employed by the IWGC as a Light Car Driver, having served during the war as a private in the Army Service Corps, in a Motor Transport unit. The IWGC had an office in Vicenza at that time, and among other things the staff were supervising the transfer of bodies from small community cemeteries in the vicinity, including the Vicenza Jewish Cemetery and the town cemetery at Origiano in the Valle dell'Agno, to the Dueville site. William Herron may have died in the Vicenza civil hospital, as by October 1919 the only British medical facility in Italy appears to have been No 38 Stationary Hospital, near Genoa.

The cemetery ceased to be used by the British at the end of 1919, and was shortly afterwards taken into the care of the Imperial War Graves Commission. During the Second World War the local inhabitants maintained the cemetery, for as one said to a colleague of the author:

> The men buried here were not involved in that later war, and some of us lost sons in Africa and Russia, and we hoped that someone there would do to their graves what we were doing to those of the British boys.

There is a small mystery in this cemetery. At the rear of the British graves there are two simple stone crosses. They mark the graves of two French soldiers, Soldats Louis Brillet and Louis Mellet, 4e SIM (thought to be 4th Section d'Infantrie Munition, a divisional ammunition handling unit) and the stone crosses are simply engraved with *mort pour le France le 3 1 1918*. The original Cemetery Register notes: *There are four French....soldiers buried in the extension,* but the layout map in the Register shows a line of six graves, and what may be one plot for several bodies, but now there are only two crosses. Were the bodies of the others repatriated to France in 1923, when, for example, on 23 January 217 bodies from the *Vicenza Cimitero*

CWGC Cemetery Dueville FM

Municipale, and probably several hundred more from other sites in the Veneto, were returned to their native soil? Despite inquiries in France, and with the CWGC, nothing had come to light about this mystery as of March 2002, and probably never will, but the search will continue.

CWGC Cemetery Dueville, the two French graves, 1993 FM

Montecchio Precalcino CWGC Cemetery

Turn left out of the Dueville cemetery car park and at the traffic lights look for a CWGC sign pointing to the left. Turn left and follow the road for 4 kilometres or so to ***Montecchio Precalcino***. The road leads to one end of a long street running off to the right; turn left. The town cemetery, the *Cimitero Communale*, is about 150 metres on the right, and the CWGC cemetery on the far side. There is small car park outside the main cemetery.

This is a beautiful little site, especially in the early summer when the walls are covered with wisteria. The cemetery was opened in April 1918, and contains 429 graves, mainly those of men who died of wounds or disease in a CCS in the village, or in accidents in the foothill dumps and workshops, or in other ways, one of which is described below. The cemetery holds the remains of a fascinating cross-section of men from the British Empire who served and died in Italy. Scotland, England, Ireland (Squadron Sergeant Major Gordon Earl Fletcher from Dublin); Wales, Monmouth (which the inhabitants were quick to point out was in neither Wales nor England). Gunner Ernest Sidney Daleymount, RFA, of The Wain, Llanfuchfu, Caerleon, Monmouth, died on 25 December 1918; on the Isle of Man, which is part of Great Britain but not of the United Kingdom; Pte H Delaney, RASC, died 2 December 1918, age 26, son of James and Elizabeth Delaney, St Johns, Isle of Man. From the Empire: two Maltese privates called Micallef, Antonio and Giovanni, numbers 217 and 207, of the Maltese Mining Company. There are aircrew from across Canada: Captain William Carrall Hilborn DFC, 45 Squadron RAF, died 26 August 1918, age 20, son of Stephen Lundy Hilborn and Josephine Elizabeth Hilborn, Quesnell, British Columbia; Lieutenant Charles Philip Uhrich, 28 Squadron, RAF, died of accidental injuries, 24 June 1918, age 24, son of Philip and Annie Urhich, Winkler, Manitoba; Lieutenant William

CWGC Cemetery Montecchio Precalcino, summer 1996 FM

Neil Hanna, 36 Squadron RAF, died of accidental injuries, 20 November 1918, age 23, Sarnia, Ontario, and Second Lieutenant Réné Hector Lefebvre, 66 Squadron RAF, died 13 April 1918, age 22, son of Barthélemi and the late Justine Lefebvre, Montreal, Quebec. There is one lone representative of the South African Military Forces, Major Atholl Murray-Macgregor MC, South African Heavy Artillery, attached 172nd Siege Battery, Royal Garrison Artillery, died 7 December 1918 age 34. (Another South African is buried in Mattarello Community Cemetery, south of Trento, in the Val d'Adige; Lieutenant William Lennox Vorster, 139 Squadron RAF, killed in action 23 July 1918, age 24, son of Hendrik Adriaan Vorster and Anna Susanna Vorster, of Vereeniging, Transvaal, South Africa. Also buried there is Williams' Observer, Serjeant Herbert George Frow, of London).

Montecchio Precalcino cemetery also contains the grave of 6728 Private H Ackroyd, 2/Border, died 2 April 1918, age 34. During April 1918, the Battalion was in billets at Camisino, a small village in the foothills, below Bydand Corner. The War Diary entry for 5 April 1918 records, *Military funeral for No. 6728 Pte H Ackroyd accidentally drowned in the ASTICO Aqueduct on 2nd Ap. The Drums played the Dead March in Saul. First Military Funeral since 1915.* Private Ackroyd is one of several men who are registered as died of drowning and buried in these two cemeteries. In *Over The Top*, an account of life in the ranks of 2/1 HAC in France and Italy, Arthur Lambert, when writing of his time in the foothills in April 1918, notes that *An aqueduct that crossed the river Astico at Camisino was in great request by men visiting the villages on the other bank.* [Chiuppano and Carrè, north of Thiene]. *It saved a long walk, but as the footpath was only a foot wide, some men under the influence of drink fell in and were drowned, and an armed guard became necessary.* There is still an aqueduct across the Astico below Camisino, according to a map published in 1998, in the same location as one shown in a British Army one of 1918, but it looks to be a steep scramble down, and back up, so it is only for the truly dedicated tourist.

Early editions of the Cemetery Register contain a tantalizing reference: *Outside, on the north, are the graves of four American soldiers, who died here in October and November 1918.* The War Diary of the DDMS (Deputy Director of Medical Services) GHQ BEF(I) records a meeting on 15 October with a US Army Medical Officer, a Major E. Ball, regarding burial of US personnel who died in US Army Hospital No 102 (in Vicenza) in the British Cemetery at Montecchio Precalcino. The reference to 'outside' also encompasses *a second Austrian plot*, and it is probable that the non-Empire dead were about to be moved to national cemeteries. No further information has so far been located. One suggestion is that the dead were disinterred and reburied at a US Cemetery in France, another that they were returned to the Continental USA in zinc coffins, in accordance with US custom. During the Great War the practice was introduced of allowing families the right to request that their fallen man should be buried in the country where he died. Ex-President Theodore Roosevelt added impetus to this move when he requested that his son, Lieutenant Quentin Roosevelt, should be buried near where he met his death in France, saying simply, '*Where the tree falls, let it lie*'. Around 47,000 bodies were returned to the Continental US, and 30,000 were buried in Europe, in eight major cemeteries, six in France and one each in Belgium and the United Kingdom.

During the late 1990s and in the year 2000, around Remembrance Day, the Grand Cross was decorated with a Union Flag, and vases of flowers placed on the War Stone by members of the local chapter of the ANF, the *Associazione Nazionale del Fante* (National Infantry Association)*;* a fine touch, much appreciated by British visitors laying poppies.

In the top right hand corner of the cemetery there is one poignant and lonely grave, that of Narain Singh, registered as an: *Indian Civilian. Released Prisoner of War. Died 20 November 1918.* His grave receives a chrysanthemum.

POSTSCRIPT
Vive l'Americani!

Introduction

On 6 April 1917 the United States of America entered the war as an 'Associated Nation' of the Allies. One infantry regiment, the 332nd, served in Italy, along with several supply and medical units. In addition, a number of American Red Cross (ARC) and YMCA personnel provided care and comforts to the Italian Army, and later to the 332nd Infantry, its support units and the US Military Mission. A very small number of American doctors served in Italy in the ranks of the British Army as unit (infantry battalion, artillery regiment) Medical Officers, but by late November 1917 most had been returned to France to join the American Expeditionary Force. At that time the USA was still not at war with Austria; *that occurred* in 7 December 1917. There were exceptions, for example Captain S Bayne-Jones US Army Medical Corps served with 11/Sherwood Foresters in France and Italy and was with the unit on the Montello and (briefly) the Asiago Plateau.

In addition to the 332nd and the ARC men (and women), a number of US trainee pilots were sent to Italy under the inspiring leadership of Fiorello La Guardia, at that time a lawyer and recently-elected Congressman for the 14th District of New York, who had learned to fly in 1915 and managed to go solo. In addition, significant numbers of immigrants returned to Italy as recalled reservists or volunteers for the Italian Army. Apart from those killed in fighting along the Austrian frontier and in accidents, some were killed at sea. In January 1916 an

Captain Fiorello La Guardia 1918

Italian merchant ship, the *Brindisi*, was crossing the Adriatic with war materials and food for Italian and Serbian forces in Albania. She was also carrying several hundred Italian-American volunteers for service with the Italian Expeditionary Force in that country. The *Brindisi* hit a mine and sank with the loss of over two hundred lives, many of them the luckless volunteers. The mine had been laid by the German UC14 which was operating against Allied shipping in the Adriatic despite there being no state of war between Italy and Germany until August 1916.

332nd IR sleeve patch. Lion of San Marco, symbol of the Veneto Province. *'Peace to you, Mark my evangelist'.*

In April 1917 the Army of the USA (AUS) was very small, scattered around the Continental US, the Philippines and other outposts. It was recovering from punitive action along the Mexican border, the Pancho Villa affair, which started in March 1916 and ended in February 1917, and was also trying to execute an emergency expansion to meet what was seen to be its inevitable involvement in the Great War. General Tasker C. Bliss, the Army Chief of Staff, was a much put upon man to cope with all those demands, but he rose to the occasion. Following the declaration of war with Germany, there was a rush of volunteers, and the AUS rapidly expanded until there were enough troops, if not enough weapons, uniforms and accommodation, to form nearly ninety divisions. Among many other things arranged rapidly by the enterprising American authorities was the establishment of eighteen training centres, each one massive by peacetime standards. As recruits arrived at the camps, they were formed into notional units and given elementary training, then formed into infantry, artillery, engineer, etc units, which were allocated numbers from a general list. For example regiments raised in Ohio during late 1917 were allocated numbers 329 through 332, and posted to the 83rd Division.

The 83rd was a New Army formation, ie not Regular (1st -7th Divisions), nor National Guard (8th-37th Divs), and manned by 'early birds', men who had rushed to join the colours when war was declared. The 83rd had been formed in August 1917 at Camp Sherman, outside the town of Chillicothe, in Ross County, southern Ohio, under the command of Major General E F Glen. The establishment was:

83rd Division

Divisional units: 83rd Div HQ Troop, 332nd Machine Gun Battalion, 308th Signal Battalion, 308th Engineer Bn

165th Brigade: Infantry: 329th IR, 330th IR, 323rd Machine Gun Battalion

166th Brigade: Infantry 331st IR, 332nd IR, 324th Machine Gun Battalion

158th Brigade: 322nd Field Artillery Regiment, 323rd FA Regt, 324th FA Regt, 308th Trench Mortar Battery.

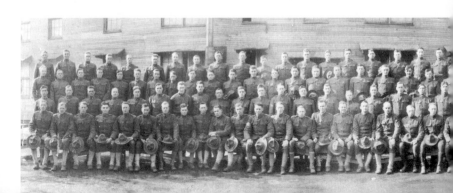

The 332nd Infantry Regiment was formed in September, around a nucleus of Colonel William Wallace, the commanding officer, and three other Regular Army officers and about thirty enlisted men. The first recruits arrived a couple of days later, on 5 September. There was a strong local element in the division, spread across many ethnic, religious and economic groups. Some of the infantry units were akin to British 'Pals battalions'. For example, Company K, 3rd Bn, 332nd Infantry, had seventy-three men, out of 250, from in and around the (then) small town of Steubenville, in Jackson County, close to the state boundaries with Pennsylvania and West Virginia. Other battalions were recruited from around the industrial cities of Akron, Canton, and Youngstown, further north, with strong contingents from Cleveland and Toledo, along with a number of extremely tough miners from the coalfields of West Virginia.

The 332nd had a difficult start. The regiment had formed in a barely completed camp just as the cold autumn rains started. It finished basic training just before Thanksgiving, and was bundled off to Camp Perry, a bleak, windswept training area on the shores of Lake Erie, near Toledo, Ohio, for small-arms training. The camp was incomplete, and torrential rain driven by howling gales soon overwhelmed the men's tents and the marquees used for dining rooms (and kitchens). The camp soon became a quagmire. Many of the recruits, instructors and kitchen staff fell ill, overwhelming the sparse medical facilities and even fewer dry buildings. One of the sick was tentatively diagnosed as having smallpox, and everyone had to be vaccinated - in the rain. After three weeks of this, just as the 332nd was about to entrain for Camp Sherman, a blizzard struck. It halted rail movement, and all but obliterated the camp. It was a tough start for the regiments, but, had they known it, excellent training for life on the battlegrounds of Europe.

The 332nd returned to the spartan surroundings of Camp Sherman, a paradise after the shores of Lake Erie. The troops were made welcome by the people of Chillicothe who opened their homes to many of the men in Camp Sherman. That gesture was especially welcome to

Company I, 2/332nd Infantry, Camp Sherman, Ohio, 26 January 1918.

332nd IR with colours inscribed. Presented by the young Italy Society of New York to the 1st Div of the USA on the Italian Front, Jan 1918.

the 332nd and for those unable to return home on furlough at Christmas or New Year. In January the division started to train in earnest for service in France, assisted by instructors with recent experience in the European Theatre of Operations, gleaned from service in the trenches with British, French, Canadian and Australian units.

During and immediately after Caporetto, many sections of the large Italian community in the US, a powerful political force, especially in the North-East, clamoured for US troops to be sent to defend their erstwhile homeland, not realising that their new country was not at war with Austria. That changed on 7 December, when the USA declared war on the Dual Monarchy. But if anything that increased the agitation. One fraternal association, the Young Italy Council of New York City, went so far as to produce two embroidered banners, to be presented to the first US unit to serve on the Italian front. The US government responded by announcing the establishment of an American Military Mission to the Kingdom of Italy, a routine matter as nearly every nation sent one to its allies. The head of the mission was Major General Eben Swift and, as with other Military Missions, it consisted of Army and Navy personnel, and diplomats, who are rarely mentioned in this context but had a vital role in ensuring, if nothing else, that any requests for help were handled in accordance with the aims and wishes of the governments involved. The mission had three specific tasks in addition to its overall 'liaison' role. First, it was to study the attitude of the Italian government, institutions and people to the Allies, their war aims and performance. Second, it was to assess the effect of German propaganda on Italy and its people and, third, it was to evaluate the Italian armed force's capabilities, equipment, morale, manpower and supply.

In February 1918, at an Allied War Conference held at Chantilly, the American delegation knew, or at least guessed, that they would be approached by the Italians about troops. General Bliss, who was heading for retirement as Chief of Staff, and was acting as President Wilson's personal representative at the conference, had recommended that the US government should avoid committing itself to involvement in the Italian campaign until accurate information had been obtained - hence the three tasks given to the Military Mission. General Bliss, and the Adjutant General, General Henry P McCain, considered that the Western Front was the critical area, and that all US resources should be concentrated there. The one exception both officers made was that an earlier promise of medical units made by the State Department should be honoured. The GOC, American Expeditionary Force, General John J Pershing, also opposed dissipating his forces, and opposed sending any troops to Italy. But a Congressional election was to take place in the autumn, and President Wilson and his team wanted to make a public acknowledgment of the role and sacrifices of Italy and the Italian people, so the Army was over-ruled, slightly. Chantilly the US delegation was approached by the Italian Prime Minister, Vittorio Orlando, seeking a 'small' force of American troops for service in Italy, as much for morale purposes as anything. The matter was referred to Washington, and hung fire until April, when the Italians again raised the matter with General Bliss, but this time with a modest request for a brigade-sized unit. The result, after more discussions and maneuverings, was that in June General Pershing was directed to transfer one regiment and supporting troops to Italy, and to despatch them as soon as possible.

The matter was not just a question of nominating units and arranging transport. When General Pershing was considering the directive, and it was not necessarily his highest priority, the March Offensive was in full swing, and he was under considerable pressure to use his forces to help stem the German onslaught. There was also the question of command and control to be considered, as he, and his government, were adamant that American troops would only operate under national command, not used in penny-packets to reinforce other nation's armies. And there was the question of logistical support. At that time France and Britain could scarcely feed themselves, so the AEF in France had to import almost every food item from the USA, process it in France and distribute it to the troops. The same thing would have to be done in Italy, using already severely taxed railway routes. By early June most of these issues had been resolved, only to be interrupted by the Battle of the Piave. It was only in early July that all the political, financial and administrative arrangements had been formalised, and the task of selecting a commander, and nominating units, was tackled by the AEF staff. They had already decided that the main component of the force would be an infantry regiment of three battalions, plus a range of supporting units in the 'Service of Supply'. The logical step was to appoint the Head of the Military Mission to command AEF(I), as he was by then conversant with the tactical and strategic situation in the theatre, and familiar with the CS, the Italian, British and French commanders, the country and its problems. So Brigadier General Charles C Treat was appointed GOC AEF(I), and his command was to be drawn from the next division to arrive in France from the US.

On 25 May the 83rd Division entrained for New Jersey, and settled into yet another new base, Camp Merrit, an enormous transit camp close to the ocean terminal at Hoboken, on the Hudson river opposite Manhattan, from where they travelled to England on the RMS (Royal Mail Steamship) *Aquitania*, once the pride of Cunard's transatlantic service. The journey took seven days, in convoy for protection against U-boat attacks, and on 15 June 1918 reached Britain.

The regiment disembarked at Liverpool and once again mounted a train. This journey took them south through the heart of England, Warwickshire, Worcestershire, Gloucestershire, men from which counties were at that time battling for their lives on an almost unknown mountain plateau, hundreds of miles away in Italy, in the battle of Asiago, part of the larger *Battaglia del Solstizio*. The 332nd, along with other units of the 83rd Division, detrained at Southampton.

They sailed for Le Havre, embarked on another train, and travelled to a staging area near Le Mans, where the 83rd Division was concentrating. There General Glen received the news that the Division was not to enter the line, but instead was to be broken up, and all but one of its units used to supply reinforcements for divisions in the line. The 332nd was sent to Italy, for reasons not yet identified, maybe it was the next in the queue, perhaps because it was the best in the Division.

The 332nd was preceded by a 2,000-strong advance party of HQ and medical staff under a Colonel Parsons which travelled to Genoa on the Italian liner *Giuseppe Verdi*, disembarking on 28 June 1918. The advance party joined the American Military Mission in Padua, and established an HQ in the city. Supply and service facilities, and a Field Hospital, AEF 331, were established near Verona, and a base hospital in Vicenza, AEF 102.

On 25 July the 332nd yet again mounted a train, stuffed into *Hommes 40* vans, and with thirty trucks and two light cars on flat-wagons. (Some officers and NCOs remained in France to attend courses at the AEF Battle Command and Supply Schools.) The regiment and support troops and their equipment had yet another slow and uncomfortable journey, brightened by the scenery and weather. Sergeant Major Joseph Lettau, the Battalion Sergeant Major (RSM) of the 3/332nd , described the scenery in his book *In Italy with the 332nd Infantry*:

Battalion Sergeant Major William L Lettau, 3rd Bn 332nd Infantry.

> *Little villages snuggled up on the mountain sides, the stone roofs sparkling in the sunshine like those of a fairy city ... We saw wonderfully constructed castles set on high peaks commanding the countryside... Not only were the castles strongly built, they were beautiful as well ....Mountains green from top to bottom, many of the peaks snow-capped. We reached Montmelain. This town was of special importance to us because here in the mountains the English had established a washing station.* [A *halt repas*, one of about a dozen on the Lines of Communication between northern France and Italy, manned by a six soldiers, assisted by local labour at peak times, with washing, toilet and water-boiling facilities.] *Our train stopped, and everyone got off and enjoyed a wash or a shave. Hot coffee was furnished and we had our noon-day meal. At Modane we stopped and Red Cross*

332nd IR, welcomed to Italy with coffee and American doughnuts, courtesy of the American Red Cross. Note hats.

representatives distributed bars of chocolate and hot coffee with rum in it, all of which were thankfully received on this cold morning.

The train arrived at Milan on 28 July, in the middle of the afternoon, and the welcome received by the troops compensated for the rigours of the journey. Hundreds of excited Italians cheered the doughboys, and showered them with flowers and fruit, while politicians made long and elegant, if incomprehensible, speeches.

The train eventually stopped at Villafranca di Verona, a small town on the Via Postumia, some 20 kms south-west of Verona. Here the troops received an 'American' welcome; fresh doughnuts and hot coffee, served by young American women, working for the American Red Cross. American pilots, under training with Italian units, flew low overhead and performed aerobatics; a splendid welcome to Italy. As a point of interest, the 332nd retained their peaked hats throughout the tour in Italy, the only US troops in Europe to do so, according to some sources.

After that unexpected treat, the troops moved by truck to their billeting areas. The Regimental HQ, HQ Company and 1/332nd were in Sommacampagnia; the 2/332nd alongside AEF 331 in the ancient town of Custozza; the 3/332nd and the Supply Company remained at Villafranca, and the Machine Gun Company was nearby, on its own in the Villa Contini, a large but uncomfortable country house. The billets were not only scattered over a large area, making control difficult, but also dirty and verminous, and with poor water supplies. The area had been used by successive waves of Italian and French troops, and had suffered all the problems of short stay tenancies. To add to these problems, the supply system was not fully operational, so the food and cooking arrangements were inadequate. If that was not enough for the

Pvt Wilbert D Macer, C Co, 332nd Infantry, 83rd Division, October 28, 1893-August 11 1918.

harassed staff, dysentery appeared and the 332nd suffered its first casualty, Private Wilbert D. Macer, age 25, of Evansville, Indiana. He enlisted in April 1918 while working as a horticulturist in Toledo, Ohio, and was posted to Company C, 1/332nd, and during his training he proved to be an expert shot with the Model 1917 Enfield rifle. He had only been in Italy a few days when he was taken ill, and on 4 August he was transferred to AEF 331, where dysentery was diagnosed. Wilbert was attended by Captain Joseph H Willis, US Army Medical Corps, who was with the soldier when he died, on 11 August. He was buried with

Air oblique photo of Italian defences south of Nervesa. The 2/332nd Bn occupied positions similar to these shown. Worcestershire Archive

full military honours in the US plot, Villafranca di Verona Community Cemetery.

Shortly after Private Macer's death, on 14 August, the 332nd was united in one billeting area, near Vallegio, on the river Mincio, south-west of Verona. Field training was carried out in the Adige valley, assisted by teams of *Arditi*. The training was imaginative and thorough; trenches, barbed wire aprons and dug-outs were constructed, and platoons and companies occupied them for four days at time, practising trench routines, including wire patrols, raids on other trenches, set-piece attacks, and defensive tactics including anti-gas drills. There were demonstrations of artillery, aircraft, flame-throwers and trench mortars. During a live firing exercise held on Friday 13 September, a set-piece attack on an 'enemy' position, supported by machine-gun, light cannon and mortar fire, there was one of those unfortunate accidents which bedevil military training at any time, in any army. The Stokes mortar crews were working as fast as they could, partly because there was group of officers observing them from immediately behind the weapons. Suddenly there was, according to Sergeant Major Lettau, *'a terrible explosion. One of the mortar shells, it was thought, exploded prematurely, scattering death and injury for many yards.'* The explosion was possibly the inevitable result of over-enthusiasm by a mortar crew, who dropped one shell down the barrel

2/332nd Infantry, Piave Front, summer 1918. Visit by Samuel Gompers.

before the other had been fired, causing both to explode, along with the propellant charge of one or both, spreading shrapnel and bits of the ruptured barrel around like the swath of a scythe. The blast killed five soldiers (one officer and four enlisted men), and wounded forty-seven officers and men.

In August the 2/332nd Battalion deployed into the front line along the Piave, coming under control of the Italian 37th Division. The battalion occupied trenches near the village of Candelù, with a rear detachment in Varago, villages south of Maserada. The sector was very quiet, and there were no casualties from enemy action.

The US troops had their share of visitors. In August Colonel Wallace and his officers entertained the Prince of Wales to lunch. The Prince being favourably impressed by his hosts and their troops. He found them to be very good company, and that they were all fit and keen. On 14 October the Right Honorable Samuel Gompers, veteran trade unionist and the President of the American Federation of Labor and member of the US Commission of Council of National Defense, visited the regiment. The band played in his honor and he reportedly smiled at the sound of familiar "rag-time" tunes. Gompers spoke to the troops on the value of teamwork. He also apparently visited the front line along the Piave, as shown in the accompanying photograph, although from the relaxed air and dress of the party it may have been taken in a training area.

Another factor in not deploying the 332nd into the front line in Italy earlier were two proposals made by Admiral William Sims, the senior US Navy officer in Europe, for amphibious expeditions in the Adriatic.

Both proposals involved a large (one source states 20,000) force of Marines, and related to anti-U-boat campaign. The first proposal was a series of landings in the vicinity of the Austrian submarine base at Cattaro, in what is now Montenegro. The second was to be in support of an Italian offensive against the Austrian-held Malakastria Heights overlooking the Albanian port of Valona. In the end nothing came of these proposals.

The 1/332nd and 3/332nd did not enter the forward, combat, zone until October, when they joined the 2/332nd near Treviso, as part of the Italian 37th Division, XI (It) Corps, of Tenth Army. Their movements and operations are not described, but it is intended to cover them in the future.

TOUR M:
AMERICANS IN THE VENETO, JUNE- SEPTEMBER 1918
Start: A4/A31 Junction
*Maps: LAC **Verona**, and **Treviso***

Itinerary: This is something of a do-it-yourself tour, as in the late 1990s there appeared to be no trace to be found in any of the communities of the brief stay by the 332nd and its support units. The best thing to do is head **west** along the A4 to the Sommacampagna exit, and explore the area using the names from this guide.

The same applies for the area along the Piave where the 2/332nd spent some weeks in trenches. Head east on the **A4** to the **A27** and leave at the Treviso Nord exit.

The roads in and around Maserada are, or were, as indicated above, poorly sign-posted, and trying to find Varago can be difficult; it is off

Men of 2/332nd Infantry in support line shelters, Piave Front, summer 1918.

Sacrario Militare, Fagarè Della Battaglia.

to the left of the road from Salettuol, and it is a question of persevering. There appears to be nothing to show for the American presence in 1918, but one local mentioned that a small number of American visitors had been that way over the recent years, all looking for some trace of the stay of the 332nd in the village.

Even more elusive is the site of the front line sector held by the 2/332nd Infantry. The few photographs located by the author show soldiers occupying dugouts burrowed into a *bund*, with a ditch alongside. The best guess, and it is no more than that, is that this was a support line (note firing step on the left), in a position laid out in similar fashion to the one in the accompanying photograph. The location of the US sector was possibly in the vicinity of Candelù, a small village set in farmland and orchards close to the bund and not far below the bottom end of the *Grave di Papadopoli*. Ask in the village, but avoid Monday afternoons in winter, when there seems to be an extra long lunch break. There is an interesting looking cemetery, but even that was very firmly closed.

Have a good rummage around the country lanes leading towards the old *bund* and the Piave, the local farmers are pleasant and fascinated to think that foreigners have even heard of their quiet corner of Italy.

From Candelù it is only a short drive **south** to the *Sacrario Militari* at Fagarè, which is on the **SS53** west of the Piave. This memorial contains the only American grave located in Italy by the author at the time of writing this guide.

Fagarè

Turn right on to the **SS53**; the Sacrario is short distance along on the right hand side, but the car park is on the opposite side of that very busy road. Opening hours are 0900-1200 hrs, and 1600-1900 hrs (summer); 1400 hrs-1700 hrs in winter. Entry is free. The *Sacrario* does not appear to receive many non-Italian visitors, although in the late 1990s the pleasant and helpful custodian indicated that there was a steady trickle of Hemingway *aficionados*, drawn to the grave of the man on whom Frederick Henry, the principal character in *A Farewell to Arms,* is supposed to have been based. The mortal remains of Lieutenant Edward N McKey, of New York, are immured in the left hand wall of the main hall of the Sacrario. On a plaque nearby is a short, enigmatic poem, **Ucciso- Piave 16 Guigno 1918**, (*Killed - 16 June 1918*) written by Hemingway and dedicated to his colleague. [It cannot be reproduced here for copyright reasons.]

Fagare. Lt Edward McKey; place of commemoration.

Lt Edward McKey, American Red Cross

Edward McKey was serving in Italy with the American Red Cross, and was killed by enemy artillery fire on the morning of 16 June 1918 in the vicinity of **Pralongo di Monastièr**, a tiny crossroads village between Monastièr di Treviso and Fossalta di Piave, on the west bank of the river. (During the Great War personnel serving with the ARC in the war zone wore army-style uniforms, and held army ranks.) Edward McKey served on the Asiago Plateau, providing amenities for Italian troops. He was responsible for the design and introduction of a mobile solid-fuel cooker, a US-Italian version of the German *gulaschekanone*, horse-drawn cookers, where food was cooked by slow heat as the vehicle followed, or travelled to, the troops. Edward was described by some Italians as *immusonito*, unsmiling, but he certainly seems to have made front line life more tolerable for many soldiers with his *cuccinetta ambulanti*.

A Farewell to Arms provides a vivid account of the fighting in Italy during what one US historian, George G Cassar, described in 1998 as the **Forgotten War**. Hemingway's descriptions of the scene are riveting. The first two pages in particular seem to the writer of this guide to capture the feel of the country, and of the

Lt McKey's damaged *cuccinetta* **at Pràlongo di Piave, post 16 June 1918.**

The Museo Storico at Rovereto.

futility of war, exactly. Perhaps this guide will make the Italian campaign less forgotten.

In Bassano del Grappa there is an interesting museum devoted to Hemingway's service in Italy: *Museo Storico* Hemingway Grande Guerra, open on Sundays between May and September; via Ca' Errizzo.

Finally,

TOUR N
Garda, Caprino, Rovereto, Mattarello

From the A4/A31 junction a fast run along the A4 *Serenissima* to the A22/E45 Brennero and up to the *Affi/Lago di Garda Sud* exit leads to the town of *Garda*. *Caprino* can be reached by way of *Costermano*. Caprino is a pleasant resort-cum-market town in the lee of Monte Baldo; the training area was on the slopes to the north of the town. Be warned that in July and (especially) August, this area is very crowded.

A short drive up the A22 leads to Rovereto and the museum mentioned earlier. From there it is another short drive up the **SS12** to **Mattarello** (two CWGC graves). A side road from Mattarello brings the tourist to the **SS349**, which becomes the **SS350** which leads directly to the northern end of the A31, and back to the junction with the A4.

Enjoy your travels, in the imagination or the driving seat.

FURTHER READING

Titles in bold are currently available

Atkinson, CT *The Seventh Division in the Great War*, London 1927
Barnett, GH *With the 48th Division in Italy* Edinburgh 1923
Baynes. J *The forgotten victor: General Sir Richard O'Connor, KT, GCB, DSO, MC* London 1989
Carrington, CF *The War Record of the 1/5 R. Warwickshire Regt* Birmingham 1923
Caddick-Adams, P *By God they can fight!: History of 143 Brigade* Shrewsbury, 1997
Cassar, George H *The Forgotten Front, the British Army in Italy 1917-1918* London, 1998
Corbett, Edward *1/8 Worcestershire* Private. Worcester 1920
Crosse, EC *The Defeat of Austria as seen by the Seventh Division* London 1919
Crutwell, C *The War Service of the 1/4 Royal Berkshire Regt (TF)* Oxford 1922
Dalton, H *With British Guns in Italy* London 1919
Dopson, FW *The 48th Division Signals in the Great War* Bristol (private) 1938
Edmonds, JE *Official History of the War Military Operations Italy* 1915-1919 London 1986
Eberle, VF *My Sapper Venture* London 1973
Fowler, S *Army Service Records of the First World War*, London, 1997
Gladden, Norman *Across the Piave* IWM London 1959
Glover, M *That Astonishing Infantry: The History of the Royal Welch Fusiliers, 1689-1989* London 1989
Goldsmid, CJH *Diary of a Liaison Officer in Italy 1918* London 1920
Halpern, PG *The Naval War in the Mediterranean 1914 -1918* London, 1987
Herwig, HH *The First World War, Germany and Austria-Hungary 1914-1918* London 1997
Hody, EH, *With the 'Mad 17th' to Italy* London 1920
Hussey, AH *The Fifth Division in the Great War* London, 1921
James, L *The History of King Edwards Horse* London 1923
***Lambert, A Over the Top* London 1922 7 2002**
Lettau, JL *In Italy with the 332nd Infantry* Youngstown, Ohio 1921
***Mackay, F Asiago, 15/16 June 1918 The Battle in the Woods and Clouds* Barnsley, 2001**
Mockler-Ferryman, AF *The Oxfordshire and Buckinghamshire LI Chronicle 1917-18* Oxford 1923
Pickford, P *War Record of the 1/4 Oxf & Bucks LI* Banbury 1919
Sandilands, R *The 23rd Division 1914-1918* Edinburgh 1923
Speakman H From *A Soldier's Heart* Abingdon Press USA 1919
Stacke, HFM *The Worcestershire Regiment in the Great War* Kidderminster 1929
Walker, G Goold (ed) *The HAC in the Great War 1914-1919* London 1930
Ward, S *Faithful: The Story of the Durham Light Infantry* London 1962
Wilks, J & Wilks, E *The British Army in Italy 1917-1919* Barnsley 1998
Wilks, J & Wilks, E *Rommel and Caporetto October, 1917* Barnsley 2001
Wyrall, R E *The Gloucestershire Regiment in the War 1914-18* London 1931

INDEX

Underlining indicates a photograph.